FINDING MY WAY:

AN AMERICAN MAVERICK IN CHINA

David M. Raddock

ISBN: 978-0-578-09347-5

ACKNOWLEDGMENTS

This is a different sort of memoir. It is a very personal story about myself as a man who spent years studying China and the Chinese language and then found this career path had allowed him to interact with China and the Chinese people from the perspective of different roles.

Learning about the ways in which my own personality intervened in the process was at times amusing and at times very painful. Writing this book was a truly private enterprise. It is now meant to illumine what it is like in the deeper but even routine sense of getting along in mainland Chinese society.

My wife Annette and frequent China traveler read the manuscript at least twice closely. I took all her suggestions very seriously and was glad that she could flesh out a few details that had eluded me and correct so many of my errors. She absorbed a good part of the stress of this project.

I am grateful also to the brighter students on the 2008-2009 International Affairs Committee of the Conference on World Affairs in Colorado. My nephew Steven Ross Keith, Steve Barr at Lynne Rienner Press, Margaret Petee Olsen, my cousin Robert Metz and my literary cousin Professor Paul Levitt of the University of Colorado, Alan C. Lopez who goes back a while, and my newly rediscovered friend Professor Mel Gurtov, Emeritus at Portland State University and formerly a compiler of The Pentagon Papers at the Rand Corporation.

Nancy Mann did some light line editing for me and Mark Hooper, at his computer in Spain, tentatively undertook the formatting and final editing. My dogs, Maggie and Benny, barked incessantly and are at least partly responsible for any errors.

TABLE OF CONTENTS

INTRODUCTION

One of my earliest childhood memories was my mother instructing me to play alone in the sandbox by digging with my little shovel until I got to China. She bought me children's books about the Chinese and the Forbidden City, and I continued to dig. I never really lost my interest either in digging or in plumbing the depths of China. And when it came to choosing a college major, I discovered "Asian Studies" in the catalog. Still naïve enough to believe that I would have to write Chinese with a brush and carry a tune to speak the language, I saw an adventure ahead.

FROM DIFFERENT VANTAGE POINTS

In my father's words, "What will you do with Chinese and your knowledge of China?" It was a sign of the times ("relevancy" was about to emerge as an issue) that I even had to justify my course of study. In the work years to follow, between the 1960s and the 1990s, I was to learn what I could about Chinese, Chinese people, and Chinese government, history, and culture.

I most appreciated "Communist China" when it was relatively closed to the West. I liked to read Chinese newspapers (between the lines), to speculate in an educated way what personalities had fallen or risen in the Politburo ("esoteric communications"), to see hidden references and meanings in Chinese characters and phrases. I even got a sort of pleasant chill from having to obtain a "Certificate of Origin" in Hong Kong for an arcane item that might have originated on the Communist mainland.

Sinicized, as a graduate student I became a "China watcher" perched in a research center in colonial Hong Kong, observing developments from afar and rubbing shoulders with the CIA (nonofficial cover) and the old sidelined generation of opinion-makers from pre-revolutionary China. I looked for new ways to meet fresh interviewees who had literally swum against the current in shark-infested waters to get from south China to Hong Kong's New Territories. These young people, many of them former Red Guards, were essential to my doctoral work on the psychological motivation of Chinese adolescents.

After several years as a professor of political science, I made the transformation to director of international political affairs for a multinational oil and energy corporation. I put on a hardhat, climbed on platforms, and walked in the hot sun with the geologists and drilling experts through oilfields in inner China for two months. Ten years later, I took on the role of independent academic, in-depth interviewer, and psychological analyst and settled in an office at the Shanghai Academy of Social Sciences, examining some of China's new youth for very subtle changes in attitude and behavior. Ultimately, on the verge of retirement from active work on China, I found myself taking up the scepter of country advisor to an American political delegation to Beijing and Eastern China.

While I was moving through all these dissimilar contexts involving different sorts of interactions with a range of Chinese people and elites, Chinese society and infrastructure were evolving stylistically. But in spite of development and modernization, one constant social dynamic continued to trouble me: the natural Chinese inclination toward hierarchy, obeisance to authority, and a resistance to the sort of individualism that Americans often take for granted.

A LOVE-HATE RELATIONSHIP WITH CHINA

As I bounced from one stepping-stone to another in my career development and my personal perspectives, China had "opened its doors" to the U.S. and the West in the early 1970s. We were learning more about the mainland Chinese, and they were learning about us. Apart from the promise of a vast market and conditions for investment and trade, China offered a certain allure that made American and other foreign businessmen go further than with other countries. We became willing to offer technology transfer as a *quid pro quo* for potential contracts, provide financing, and take the risk of dealing with the unknown for a crack at a pot of gold. The American entrepreneur would risk giveaways, joint ventures, the Chinese lack of familiarity with management techniques, a Communist government still making its way into the mainstream of free market practices, and legal confusion. I bought some penny stocks on the Shanghai stock market and lost all the money in the spirit of adventure. If the Chinese could dine on *xiangrou*, or dog (head staring at its master from the lazy Susan), many of us took a bite along with them, pace the Humane Society.

We looked to China as a potential laboratory for ecological development and as a window on a whole new branch of homeopathic medicine. Red Guards rampaging through the streets and fighting each other in the name of Mao Zedong were frightening in their violence and fanaticism, but not a few of us embraced the whole youth culture in the People's Republic.

Like other Westerners, I had a love-hate relationship with China and the Chinese. It was colored by my own expectations, prejudices, and fantasies. And it was contaminated by the concept of a new generation of educated "China specialists" — myself among them — who developed a unique mental prism for seeing through the haze and nonetheless often managed to guess wrong.

THE SHAPE OF THE BOOK

The self-contained stories in this book of China memoirs share a common thread, a personal tension with which the reader might identify. When I came to work on projects in China, my perspective changed over time and was shaped by my varying roles. I struggled to cut through the dazzle of Western-style modernization, archetypes, the abstraction of human rights violation, and the unfairness of China's ironic economic manipulation of the U.S. My different functions and personal interactions in Chinese organizations and society are likely to inform the reader not only about China but also about me. My own efforts to get along with the Chinese stand out in a singular way from one story to another. In the end, I reconcile the images I have of China and the Chinese with my own behavior and growth. Could it be that the Chinese are more accepting and positively responsive to me than some rigid and intolerant elements who might call themselves my "fellow Americans?"

CHAPTER ONE

1960-1961

RED SQUARE

At the age of nineteen, on a wintry December day in Moscow's Red Square, I met a Muscovite who might have stepped out of a Tolstoy novel. I was in Khrushchev's Soviet Union as a member of the Cornell University Glee Club. It was my first trip internationally except for vacations in Nassau and Bermuda with my family. Now, I would be singing, actually performing, on the cultural exchange. We had been selected to entertain in a new era of detente and peaceful coexistence. The inauguration of John Kennedy would take place in weeks.

A gnarled old man, with a wily, provocative smile, approached me. He looked in my eyes and said, "Zdravstvuytye," spitting out the word.

I greeted him back and smiled. I had only begun to study Russian in school. This Russian old-timer, bearded down to his chest, looked like a grandfatherly type from a Tolstoy novel (someone who might let his vodka trickle down his chin while he burst into a *kazakhskiy* on the dining room table). Pointing flamboyantly at St. Basil's Cathedral next to the Kremlin, he remarked to me, "Before the revolution, the church was the weapon of Czarist oppression!"

As I strived to answer him, I looked around. "In the U.S., we have freedom of religion," I protested.

More Russians were walking over toward us out of curiosity to catch a word or two or to glimpse what was transpiring. I had always liked an audience when I performed in theater. As a participant in summer stock, I had acted onstage before smaller turnouts.

Looking behind me, I realized I was standing in the shadow of the statue of Minin and Pozharsky. I mounted the base of the monument and tried my best to project my voice to the crowd surrounding me. Without regard for decorum, I wanted our conversation to reach as many as possible. The old man who started the debate had no intention of climbing on this icon with me. He remained at ground level and just grinned up at me.

In faltering, first-year Russian, I tried to articulate the thought that in the U.S. we enjoyed separation of church and state. But just as I was realizing that my Russian wasn't advanced enough to express my thoughts, a number of men in black coats, together with our chief Soviet handler, broke out from the dense gathering. They then proceeded to shoo and shove away the common people, with a touch of gentility only as an afterthought.

Many of the folks lingered waiting for me to find the right words, willing to take the risk of being laggards in the face of the KGB. The older initiator of the discussion didn't budge until the plainclothes security pulled him away.

Was this my "five minutes" of glory in the second phase of the Cold War? I hadn't done a very good job. Few heard me, and more likely, the rest didn't understand me. It had been impromptu, and at least I had the presence of mind to mount a stone base where people could see me. (Some could argue that I made a fool of myself.) As I got down from my monumental "soapbox," the Glee Club conductor, Professor Sokol, came out from the Kremlin Museum. "David, what on earth were you doing up there?"

I was the lone student in the Glee Club who spoke Russian and treated the dormitory students to the cognac I had bought during a layover in Amsterdam. Fortunately, the Russian undergraduates drank fast. Over the next two weeks, I went off in separate directions with my buddy, a West Indian graduate student who was involved in a number of incidents in both Moscow and Leningrad. He picked up a nineteen-year-old out-of-towner at the museum, and she took us on a forty-five-minute public bus ride to what looked like the outskirts of Moscow to her aunt's apartment. There, we had a private lunch of *shchi* (a watery, tomato-based soup with cabbage) and black bread. In the interest of my buddy's friendship with the girl, we didn't let politics undermine his budding love. I believed this was a set up that the Soviets designed to impress us.

In retrospect, if the Russian authorities had needed to create an embarrassing diplomatic incident, I was an easy target. One might argue that I had embarrassed myself — simultaneously doing myself a disservice — by selling my underwear for rubles to a man who showed me the orthodox synagogue in Moscow. When an unemployed and politically hassled engineer implored me to deliver a letter to U.N. Secretary-General Dag Hammerskjöld, I ignored the risks and his own racist remarks and stuck it in my vest pocket.

In all these foolish antics, I could rationalize that I was only a college kid looking for excitement. I could reflect that I had been exposed to the ideologically and culturally dissonant, and I had practiced skills that would serve me well in an international career. In truth, I welcomed confrontation and action. Some years later, when I came to look at my behavior in a more self-critical way, I learned that no less a political figure than Bobby Kennedy at about the same age had lectured from the Bible, also in Red Square. No one had instructed me specifically, but, singing apart, wasn't I supposed to further the interest of peaceful coexistence with the Soviet students and others I met?

Seeing more of the world definitely brought out the grandiosity in me. Trying to do something about what I saw was like leaving my own special imprint.

CHAPTER TWO

1963-1964

TAIWAN BY THE CHINA SEA

At Cornell University, I gradually leaned toward pursuing a career in teaching international politics — Chinese and Soviet. I rationalized that I could perform in a larger lecture hall onstage (I envisioned myself in the Ivy League, of course), adding my own brand of wit and entertainment, and I would be doing cerebral work. I assured my father, who measured success in money, that I could earn a lot doing research on China on contract with the government. I skipped the idea of law school and relegated theater to a hobby.

By my senior year, I had received a Carnegie grant to study Chinese language in Taiwan (at that time called Formosa or the Republic of China). I was to be there for a year after graduation and couldn't leave for East Asia soon enough. I went via Hong Kong. The colony was then a diversion for me — an anachronism of colonial and treaty port China where people referred to mainland China as "Mao Zedong's place." The main debate at the tailor shops was whether China ever would act against Britain's occupation by treaty and lease of the New Territories. I dallied in Hong Kong's decadence, and I definitely left my mark in the wrong places. But I wasn't in the Far East to have a good time. I was anxious to get to Taiwan, socially and aesthetically in many ways a throwback in 1963 to the

China *before* the revolution—a Disneyland of traditional China.

I have often since expressed my disdain for Chinese *keqi*—flattery, being too kind in a political way—in the Chinese system of language and social grace. It often seemed like it masked anger or represented a defense against aggression. Whatever, it was "phony." But from time to time, when I've needed a dose of confidence or my self-esteem has registered below normal, I have welcomed a bouquet from a Chinese. One can be discouraged so easily from trying one's command of the French language in France. But in Taiwan, if I stumbled over a few words in Chinese when meeting someone, I could always expect the Chinese person to flatter my use of the language. In fact, he could raise me from the level of a beginner to an accomplished linguist. Of course, once I became the recipient of a generous comment like, "You speak better than me," I had to search my inventory of *keqi* phrases like " *na-li na-li*" (it's nothing), "*bu gandang*" (you flatter me), or the more nonchalant or cynical "*Ni tai keqi*" (you're too polite) if my words had been altogether too rudimentary.

I enjoyed Taiwan for its native Taiwanese population, its food, and its emulation—if superficial—of the old and elegant ways things were supposed to have been done in China. As for me, instead of taking a cab, I rode into Taipei from the outlying airport in a traditional pedicab—a road trip that seemed almost as long as the flight from Hong Kong.

Near my school, I located my old language instructor, whose teaching work had made it impossible for him to get a graduate degree in economics at Cornell. He had been a guest in my home in New York, and at first, I clung to him like a bridge between the familiar and unfamiliar. I wanted to blend with the people. I bristled when older American graduate students told me that I had to keep a servant in my house because it was expected of foreigners.

My one retreat from the "twenty-four/seven" program of total immersion in Chinese was the U.S. Military Officers' Club on Chungshan Pei Road (one section away from both my place and the home of top security chief Chiang Ching-kuo, the eldest son of Chiang Kai-shek). The Officers' Club theme song, "Taiwan by the China Sea," played as soon as the dancing got under way, came to grate on my nerves:

Taiwan by the China Sea, cha-cha-cha,
My true love whispers close to me,
The island of romance,
The swing and sway of dance.

I chuckled the first time I heard these strains of music in the dining room. After all, this wasn't the Bahamas again. But when I witnessed Chiang Kai-shek's playboy son rise from his table of women to "cha-cha," my stomach turned. An American haven overseas could not entertain without Westernizing and belittling its host culture. We were treating Taiwan like another one of our satellite resorts.

Since prostitutes for foreigners was neither a healthy nor socially sustaining diet, I discovered a way to mix with Chinese peers. Educated young women observed the custom of not dating one boy but hanging out in groups. An occasional Westerner could be admitted. Young women on campus usually wouldn't date boys on a one-to-one basis or they would risk being gawked at or called names. My recourse for a social life was the Jack Yu Private School for English. I taught English there and thus also held a slight aura of authority over the students, who were only slightly younger than me. In the summertime, college students seeking to improve their English conversation would enroll and theoretically learn American English. I taught these Chinese and made several new friends. My effectiveness with them even allowed me to continue part-time teaching in my home.

One girl in particular caught my attention with her long black hair, her skimpy sundress, and dark tan. I introduced Christine to many American ways and ordered her first scotch at the Officers' Club. Her face turned red with the baptismal sip of alcohol, but she soon outdistanced me. We walked unaccompanied through the streets, enduring some catcalls from strangers and pedicab drivers. We even danced to "Taiwan by the China Sea."

I was becoming a part of the family, probably by her parents' design. Her mother, who supervised the servant's cooking over a bare, gas-fuelled cook top, invited me to come over for lunch as often as I pleased. The middle-class parents, who were refugees from the mainland, had scant little to show for their earlier status except a Qi Baishi painting of shrimp and a cockroach and the unopened bottle of Johnny Walker Black Label that stood on their mantelpiece. Their house was small and modified Japanese-style.

Christine's godbrother, Henry Huang, also in my class during the summer, was a pitted-faced fellow with an unverbalized resentment toward Americans. He certainly didn't care for me. His father, the former governor of Hunan Province, now held the somewhat surreal post of Chairman of the Committee for the Planning of the Recovery of the Mainland. Slogans for retaking the mainland were all over—on the walls along streets, on billboards, and on beer labels. One thing about Taiwan was that I could observe and even be a part, yet poke fun delicately at some of their common political fantasies. I gave Mr. Huang such a hard time about how he was enjoying retirement that he began to crack jokes self-derisively about his own position. Anthropologists are participants and observers. I was part of it all and critic at the same time.

The younger brother in the Huang family, who acted like Christine's playmate, was a quiet "dissident." He knew all the social critics of the Kuomintang government and was eager to find a spot for me among the tolerated protesters. All the authority-figures in his extended family were active members of Chiang Kai-shek's Kuomintang government. If a mainland refugee had a reputable background, at most he would risk some sort of government surveillance for joining such mildly seditious discussion groups. But local Taiwanese who openly supported independence from Kuomintang control were not to be tolerated any more than Communists.

Christine's parents wanted me to be among their friends when the celebrated Mme. Chiang cut the ribbon at her charity orphanage on Yangmingshan. As a student of China who deplored some of the activities of this "Soong sister" whose wedding had made the cover of *Life* magazine, I could have excused myself. (All it would take was a little *keqi* language.) As it was, she held out her white-gloved hand, and I barely shook it. So much for militant protest. And Mme. Chiang only looked bemused.

Youth in Taiwan generally weren't very politically aware or politically active. Many feigned disinterest, but some resented the American student for his or her worldliness and political awareness. Discussion at parties often centered on poetry, with one writer — icon to his audience — leading the session. On New Year, the liquor came out, but the conversation or activity wasn't political, social, or sexual. When we all got sufficiently drunk, we resorted to games like "Does our foreign friend trust his Chinese friends?" I was pressured into falling over backward, and my friends Christine and Henry would catch me. What the hell! I let myself fall. No one caught me. Henry managed to extend his leg to break the fall, inadvertently causing me to rip the cartilage in my knee. I didn't feel the pain until I got back to my house and was unable to walk. I held on to the street wall, pushing myself up a hill to the main street, and flagged a cab to the Western missionary doctor. It was dark, but I must have looked like some of the very old ladies with bound feet who propped themselves against the wall for support.

The party of the year came on a lovely spring night. The cold in the air from Taiwan's winter was dissipating when Johnny Huang, Christine, and I stole across an empty space in front of Li Ao's house. Li Ao was a very famous social critic in Taiwan, a mainlander, who called for an opening up of the system and greater democracy. He even argued that democracy was intrinsic to Chinese culture. Most everyone sat at his feet like he was a guru. But it was getting late, and the presence of cars outside with headlights turned on and trained on the house was a conspicuous sort of surveillance that could be observed from the inside through one or two of the windows. I was getting drunk on bad liquor, there was nothing to eat, and I was tired.

We sat in a circle on the floor. "If you look at the pattern of hierarchy from the Confucian family to the emperor in traditional society, you see authoritarianism and scant little evidence of democracy cutting across the lines of authority," I declared as a challenge. Li Ao's face was red, but I guessed that it must be from the whisky.

"David," he said in Chinese, "what sort of political system do you predict will evolve here if that is the case?"

"Maybe a combination. But you're better off in any case with more of a dictatorship." My Chinese words were losing their tonal quality and faltering. Li Ao's face by now seemed a deeper red, like a tomato reaching its time for picking.

"Frank Goodnow. You're Frank Goodnow!" he exclaimed. "You want us to go backwards. You deny us the democracy you enjoy in America."

I laughed as though we were engaged in careless repartee.

"Get out!" he yelled.

"You're kidding," I said.

Li stood up, stumbled a bit, grabbed me by the back of my collar and seat of my pants, and pushed me to the front door and into the headlights. So much for exchanging views, agreeing to compromise, and collective protest.

Oddly, I was also kicked out of the U.S. Military Officers' Club only a short time later. Christine was away in Taichung at college, and I often brought along a friend from Columbia who was a schoolmate here. A hulking fellow who walked about like "Frankenstein," he tended to create a cacophony in the club by playing several slot machines simultaneously while walking around the club with his fly open. In addition, I had the misfortune of a having one of my checks bounce. When I refused to honor the request of a chief warrant officer in charge that I refrain from bringing my disruptive friend one evening, I was asked to leave — permanently. Hence, my main legitimate entertainment was now reduced to the movies.

The 1960s would be a turning point in Taiwan for political rumblings. I looked for a cause and exercised some judgment. I found an activist friend in the abstract expressionist artist Liu Kuo-sung, a calm and collected Sichuanese who had been affiliated at one time with the Central Military Academy. He never really set out to pit himself against either the culture or social order, but some right-wing traditionalist critic who taught in the military accused him and his "Fifth Moon" group of trying to undermine established norms. In one case, one of the abstract artists made a painting perhaps a bit like Franz Kline's, and the military stalwarts attacked him viciously for "obviously drawing the character Chiang" as in Chiang Kai-shek and then giving it a tilt toward the left. Thus while Khrushchev was lambasting modern artists in the Soviet Union, the arch-conservative art critics on Taiwan were accusing the Fifth Mooners of corrupting styles in art and trying to take Taiwan down the primrose path to communism.

I was stimulated by this story and began to read art books and Liu's own books about his Chinese art to expand my art history knowledge and vocabulary in art-related terminology. I wanted to tell this story. I worked on this issue in class at school, and I would meet with Liu outside to discuss his work. When Liu and the Fifth Moon group had their first major exhibition in Taipei, the biggest buyers were American professors who studied China. I bought one and then another. A year later, my article was published in the then acclaimed *Arts Magazine*. What did I know about art? The article was more about the ironies of politics. Two years later, Liu received a major American foundation grant to work in New York, and I was back in the city to welcome him.

A dreary winter, cold without proper heating, leaped into summer and did nothing to lift the spirits from what was becoming a boring environment. My expulsion from the Officers' Club left me yearning for the simple American standby foods. My main interest—politics—had receded into the background. Arguments tended to center on who would succeed Chiang Kai-shek—his older son or a more legitimate statesman in the vice presidency. I even brought my lumbering school buddy to Christine Feng's house. There, with an ordinary intake of scotch, Mr. Feng, Christine (seated on her father's lap), and I debated affairs in the U.S. When Feng happened to be curious about "base" questions like what constituted an American—that is, a *real* American—I would bristle with defensiveness. My friend Rensselaer III pointed out that whereas my relatives from two generations past were Jews who had emigrated from Russia and Poland, his own ancestors could be dated back to the Mayflower (probably a fact or legend that I could have used in arguing his case in the club). They were supposedly the originators of America and subscribed to Protestant Christianity or, still better, Episcopalianism. In vain, I argued what we had been taught in elementary and secondary school—namely, that America was a "melting pot" of nationalities and that the European immigrants were the fiber of our country. Mr. Feng *and his daughters* were more inclined to believe my friend because his message resonated with what had been ingrained in them already by missionaries. To them, although an adequate candidate for Christine's hand, I was still identified with China's minorities.

With the Officers' Club shut to me, there was little entertainment. Political discussion and activity was very limited or indirect. It came as a surprise one rainy day when I went to the movies that a grubby, middle-aged man followed me all the way to my favorite restaurant. He struck up a conversation and asked if he could join me. I had never experienced such forward behavior in Taiwan. As I dried myself and tried not to be put off by the smell of his dripping raincoat and hat, he just sat there at first asking banal questions about what I did and how I liked Taiwan. I mused that he might be an elite secret police officer or a member of the Kuomintang's sixth section for counterespionage until I became alert to the reality: he asked me to "name" Chinese persons I knew. We had left the movies! I excused myself as quickly as possible, asked him point blank if he was an undercover political cop, and then went out into the still, muggy air. Even the "spook" game had become tiresome in this flat society, a dictatorship with a hollow, silly ideology calling itself a republic.

The tentacles of the regime extended to our classes at language school. The Chinese teacher, a sensitive man who had stayed in my house in New York one Christmas, got frightened over a comment of mine in the discussion of our Chinese Communist readings. Tearfully, my friend, who had resettled in Taiwan, cast me out of his class.

CHAPTER THREE

1981

PICKLES IN CHINA

HOW I WAS OUSTED FROM CHINA

I had spent so many years studying Chinese language, as well as China's civilization, history, culture, psychology, and politics. I had even spent a year in Taiwan reading mostly Chinese and speaking only Mandarin. Was I to leave the academy altogether and squander most of this knowledge on political intelligence reports for an oil and energy services company? Enserch, a diversified multinational, did everything from recovering oil, diving offshore, and constructing power plants to working with synfuels. I developed a program to generate social environment outlook studies for projects of its subsidiaries in more than thirty countries. Most of these were undertaken from afar, but I did focused work on site for the critical ones. Most of the key host countries were in the Middle East, Africa, and Southeast Asia. With nothing for us to do yet in China, I often confused my receding Russian with my Chinese.

Of course, I tried to keep up with reading Chinese Communist newspapers, and I got an occasional kick out of startling a Chinese diplomat at a Washington party with my knowledge of Mandarin. At least I could use the language in a limited way in the Mandarin and Sichuan restaurants that were beginning to spring up in Washington and New York. I convinced myself that my use of Chinese would spur the imported chef to extra effort. One bona fide chef trained in China particularly respected my taste for *paocai*, or Chinese pickles. Once in a while, a manager would gift me with an extra plate of pickled cabbage, shriveled and soaking beckoningly in the restaurant's marinade, or an owner or manager would gravitate toward my table and join us as if we were all like family.

Occasionally, a lone waiter would take offense at my use of Chinese: the better I sounded, the worse for me. It was a loss of face for a Caucasian American to speak the national language better than an American of Chinese descent. One waiter, whom I had taken to be simply reserved, had been building anger so long that one day he spat out over my menu: "Who the hell do you think you are? Oh, you say, 'Look, there's the Chinaman bringing my food. I'll surprise him with my Chinese.' I'm as much an American as you, mister."

Usually, however, the meal and communication were palatable, and a spirit of sharing predominated. (Admittedly, years later, after I had experienced my dose of secret police oppression in the People's Republic of China, I would periodically tickle myself by walking up to visiting mainland Chinese and saying something ominous in Mandarin in a low voice.) Still, the benefits of my many years of practicing tones and learning two sets of Chinese characters (plus an additional shorthand for newspapers) were diminishing with desuetude.

For a long time, I had to put up with the irony that many of the key marketing executives in the subsidiaries, a white conservative lot from the old school of rural produce auctions, doubted my knowledge of China and Chinese. "Have you actually been there?" hollered one bombastic executive in international marketing at New York's World Trade Center as he blew cigar smoke up into the air. Despite my seven years of specialized study, my three degrees, my year in Taiwan, he preferred an American Chinese engineer to take the lead for him, someone who looked the part, dressed in a foppish, Hong Kong–made, double-breasted boiled wool suit. This ambitious young engineer, who insisted that he had influential relatives in league with the Chinese Communist leadership, brought to mind an old childhood buddy of my father who used to claim to be a Communist, denounced Wall Street from our backyard swimming pool, and fancifully bragged of his Chinese friend in a Brooklyn restaurant who had a hotline to Mao.

Of course, I'd been making cross-cultural misjudgments from the start. Once, during my tenure in Hong Kong doing doctoral research, I had applied through China Travel to be allowed into China. A young female clerk in a Mao jacket asked me if I had seen the film of the celebrations of the twenty-third anniversary of the People's Republic. I said I had seen it and enjoyed it.

"What did you like about the movie?"

Thinking like a 1960s antiwar Marcusian, I replied, "The absence of weapons in the parade." The vapid expression on the girl's face turned to surprise and then blushing shame. Mouth open, she stared at me. Searching for a quick explanation, I somehow blurted out a spontaneous couplet:

Wu qi yue duo

Guo jia yue ruo

(The more the weaponry,

The weaker the country)

But the authorities at China Travel were offended and told me to go with a group.

With the impetus that Henry Kissinger provided after the normalization of relations, it was to be expected that trade and investment opportunities in China would open up for U.S. corporations. As the Chinese quest for technology accelerated, more and more agents would emerge in Washington claiming links to Chinese insiders.

One owned a well-known, quasi-authentic Chinese restaurant on upper Connecticut Avenue frequented by Kissinger. Many did have families who had been in the patriotic front in Hong Kong and maintained ties with the mainland Party and front organizations (unbeknownst to Joseph McCarthy two decades earlier). Still others might indeed have been personal friends of the revolutionary leaders and have kept their contacts in a sort of "China closet." Some carried calling cards indicating their areas of influence. One could not deny their potential leverage in a society strung together by networks of informal relationships and extended familial ties. If your friend had been my friend, we all shared a common bond; if you and I had hung out in the early days together, we were *lao pengyou* (old friends), and the bond would persist through time and space. These informal relations could be critical in identifying a business opportunity, opening doors, and clinching a deal.

Right after normalization of relations in 1979, a team of such middlemen approached the Washington office of Enserch almost cold, referred only by a Price Waterhouse consultant on the Middle East. A former undersecretary from Nixon's and Ford's administrations and a then recent secretary of the Navy provided the opening act for the main player, a Cantonese Chinese who, it later turned out, couldn't put together even a few intelligible sentences of Mandarin.

Mr. Chan was a thin, frail-looking man of indeterminate age who seemed to form an arc from head to toe, like a Venet sculpture. When he appeared a short time later in our offices together with his advance men, he was dressed in a natty blue double-breasted blazer. The two former U.S. officials sat on either side of him as he lazily made his pitch and took questions from the two of us in attendance. Slouched against the back of the stiff sofa in my boss's office, he reminded me of a cross between the heir apparent to the throne and an opium smoker in recline.

He knew Mao Zedong and Zhou Enlai personally, he told us, through the patriotic front. His family had given money to the cause in the 1940s, and he had kept in touch afterward. He promised an invitation from the Petroleum Ministry in Beijing, and boasted that he would have an inside track on the standing committee's agenda and the voting of the National People's Congress as it met in Beijing. (Voting on what, we didn't know.) We might even meet Party Secretary Deng Xiaoping, he slyly suggested. Indeed, he assured me, we were *a shoo in* (for something-or-other). And it would cost each corporation—Enserch and W. R. Grace, partnered for the occasion—a mere million dollars plus expenses.

During the intervening months of planning and negotiation, we saw little of Mr. Chan, who must have felt that too much exposure might damage his charisma. We met with W. R. Grace team members and our own exploration and drilling people in Dallas to make our plans. Ultimately, Chan reappeared for a going-away dinner in Washington. In a surprisingly modest, nonalcoholic neighborhood restaurant in Maryland, just north of the District, we celebrated the impending journey. The owner of the restaurant brought out a battered metal teapot full of 1964 Chateau Margaux.

That summer, it was confirmed that I would accompany Enserch's petroleum exploration delegation, together with representatives of W. R. Grace, to China. We were to investigate onshore fields from one end of China to the other. Our domain: the watery and lake-pocked fields of Jiangsu in the east, and northern Sichuan's dusty terrain, which borders Tibet and resembles parts of America's mountainous far west. We would look also at the problems of secondary and tertiary recovery in the mature fields.

Instead of a previously planned safari in East Africa with my wife Annette, I soon found myself pulling out of the Beijing airport in a motorcade of small black cars. We drove along a broad avenue lined with birch trees. Mine was the last car and had been designated for the lowest rung: a consulting geologist on contract and me. The political dignitaries and Chan were piled into the first, slightly larger black car. Hierarchy was clearly important in the new China, and until the Chinese could sort us out, we traveled top-heavy.

To my surprise, we circumnavigated the main part of the capital city, where most of the hotels then were situated, and learned that instead of staying in the Beijing Hotel, we were to be placed at the Diaoyutai State Guest House, a private park with multiple dwellings for state visitors, important delegations, individuals like Henry Kissinger, and even Jiang Qing, Mao's radical wife, who was then kept under house arrest for treason and conspiracy. Except for a few workmen, laundry women, and a bunch of us who decided to jog around the lake, the grounds were very serene.

I joined the runners and soon found myself lagging behind in a hazy, aerobically deficient state. I truly tried to keep up, but this was the first time I had run fast since I told a leather-jacketed Rosalie Mazzofaggio to fuck herself in junior high school. The formation soon disappeared ahead of me.

I slowed down and ambled along the lake distracted by a brood of ducks (ah, Peking ducks, I mused) until I suddenly realized that I had no idea of the address of our lodging. All twenty or so buildings looked very much alike, and the roadway seemed to veer in different directions. The area was bereft of people. I turned around to walk back and look for markers or some sort of intervention. After going a short distance, I heard laughter ahead. Two teenage boys were smiling in my direction, and I spoke to one in Chinese.

"I'm an American with a petroleum delegation," I told

him. "I got separated from our group of oilmen getting some exercise."

At first, neither seemed to have any idea of what to do. Then the first fellow offered to help, and his friend and I followed him through twists and turns to a sloping area near the lake, where we accosted another few young workers. After they had absorbed my story through the words of the new friend I had made, they engaged in some small talk and then looked me over in earnest. The one who was friendliest with my companion grinned at him and said, "Eh, Little Mao, I didn't know you could speak English."

It was beginning to get dark. My new friend smiled and escorted me back to my building.

"I'm embarrassed," I said. "Imagine getting lost like this—like a toddler in the park." Then I thought: *Just how does this guy know right off the bat where I belong?*

At dinner in our lodge, the chef prepared a meal in which the appetizers and dishes were molded and shaped in the form of farm animals. The food looked like the peasants' paintings sold at the base of the Great Wall. Two cases packed with dry ice were placed just inside the kitchen door. They contained Dave Clary's insulin (our drilling VP was seriously diabetic and in his fifties) mixed in with an assortment of vodka and scotch and a couple of bottles of rum for Peabody, the key geologist, to mix with his Coca-Cola. We had as many courses at dinner as at the best of Chinese banquets I'd attended, and I was served up as the laughingstock for being "little boy lost."

Beijing was a pleasure to behold for a former China

scholar. Nothing much went wrong other than the ceremony surrounding a short meeting with the vice-minister of the petroleum industry and key ministry officials. As Mr. Chan took a chair in the rear corner of the room, I inadvertently sat at what was regarded at the head of the table. When the vice minister motioned me to move (Who are *you*?) and called upon Chan to take his proper place opposite him, Chan did a dizzy tap dance, blushed from self-consciousness, and addressed the vice minister in a sort of gibberish I can only liken to "chop suey."

After this introductory meeting, we walked through the pavilions of the Forbidden City, and I felt a hand on my rump. I reached behind and noticed that my wallet had been lifted from my back pocket. So much for my assumption that the Chinese would keep an eye out to protect foreign guests from foul play. The leather in this new wallet was more precious than the Chinese play money then issued (money coupons of cheap paper to protect the value of the real currency).

It was at about four in the morning some days later that our foray into the onshore oilfields began. We flew to Chengdu, Sichuan, and thence traveled overland to the arid fields in the north basin of the province, where we asked questions about soil conditions, surveyed machinery, and shared our opinions in seminar format on how to drill at different levels and other problems of production. By this time, I was assigned to ride at the back of the caravan — often alone.

It seemed that Mr. Chan had made up promotional material about us with biographical blurbs on each member of the delegation. I was described as a student of

China's society, fluent in the language, whose function was to advise Enserch about the state of politics in China and China's oil industry. My official position with Enserch, my academic background, and my work with other countries were never discussed. The consensus of the China hands I talked with later was that Mr. Chan and his cronies might as well have put a red flag next to my name and picture with "CIA" emblazoned across it.

I was pleased with the way the petroleum authorities in the northern Sichuan basin accepted, and even seemed eager for, the *pro bono* advice of Western experts. However, I managed to antagonize the translator on the Chinese side, a young woman with pigtails, whose English rendering at one point I corrected. We had done this sort of thing with exchange delegations in Washington, and the Chinese had welcomed the clarifications then. When this woman took offense instead of accepting help in the collegial Maoist fashion, I gave up idealizing the new China. Moving back east across China to Jiangsu after almost a week seemed like taking flight in more than one way.

A sunny, temperate free afternoon in Shaobo, Jiangsu, called for us to take a walk through the little town. Gregath, the senior geologist for W. R. Grace, who looked like Errol Flynn and whom we dubbed "the Commander" when he held his pipe, joined the Enserch crew in kicking up some dust along the unpaved main street.

As we sauntered along the road attracting attention, we stopped to buy some abacuses at a general store. Peabody, whose belly showed his rum and Coke, staged a competition between a Chinese kid and a member of our group, abacus against calculator. A framed photograph of the liberal Prime Minister Zhao Ziyang looked down on us. Zhao would have approved of the game, but with cautious optimism about the Chinese instrument and more concern for the boy's feelings than Peabody showed.

I was eager to get on with the walk, but as we talked idly among ourselves, I had to resist peering into the open doorways of the one- or two-room houses lining the avenue. It would have been a breach of boundaries to enter, but I couldn't suppress my curiosity, and rather than do something intrusive, I asked an elderly man smoking in a chair outside his doorway what his house was like. Open and hospitable, he led me into the living area, floors made of concrete, which his family of four considered home. Against one wall was a double-decker for his children, against the other a traditional *kang* (the stone stove/bed that provided warmth at night). I was surprised that these ordinary Chinese still rested their heads on hard ceramic pillows.

Thanking the head of the house, I caught up with my friends, lingering just outside, and we continued our stroll. As we neared the end of the road, I noticed that a coterie of children of different ages was now trailing us. My friends soon gave up playing with them, but I wheeled around and began to engage them in conversation in Chinese.

Chaos ensued. The townspeople acted as if aliens had landed. So many folks poured out of houses and the dense woods it felt like a field of prairie dogs had mobilized against us. We were pushed up close against the wall that lined the inner side of the road, fielding questions from all sides. Questions abounded and many younger people shoved their way to the front simply to touch our clothes. I enjoyed the tumult and wasn't intimidated even by the huffing-puffing of a perturbed policeman who appeared in full white uniform with braids and cap. He had come to disperse the mob, not with his stick but by blowing his whistle. He seemed embarrassed and flustered at the lack of decorum and, in freeing us, urged us essentially to mind our own business.

As we advanced a little farther to what appeared to be woodland at the end of the road, some of the stalwarts in the crowd persisted in following us. At the opening to the woods, with no uniformed law officers in sight, a much more orderly contingent of people gathered neatly before us. They waited as though they expected us to perform. Then they seized the initiative. Some older folks led off by asking whether they could query us about our country. (Was somebody subtly directing the people now?)

What visiting American wouldn't enjoy this type of experience, even when it became clear that most of the adults could speak only their native dialect? The problem was resolved when an older middle school graduate was able to translate from the local dialect to Mandarin. I represented my colleagues and myself by speaking Mandarin. Our verbal ping-pong rally ended consensually and politely.

Most of the townspeople and villagers in the group, though residents of the province's third largest city, had never met an American. A woman in her eighties, largely toothless and in a black pajama-like tunic, could recall a missionary passing through when she was a child. The same woman called after me as we turned to head back to the compound: "Are you really an American? American Chinese or American?"

I laughed. "Plain American. What makes you think I'd be Chinese?" She smiled.

Back in our dormitory, we washed for dinner and drank from our supply of alcohol. "I guess I can still handle myself well in Chinese," I reflected. But a crisis was emerging. Peabody was beginning to notice that his rum was almost all gone. I had tried to nurse my vodka because I suspected we would have the usual Chinese toasts made with the still more virulent local counterpart of the potent Maotai wine—good fuel for Molotov cocktails. (Now that I think of it, that Chinese libation might have been responsible for the reflux I developed later.)

"The rest of the liquor is running out too," Peabody said. "With four more days or more out here, 'the professor' [he meant me] is going to have to come up with some local stuff."

"Don't panic, it's not water we're running out of," I replied. "But there must be some local drink, and I'll find it. At least we'll all be able to keep our balance when we squat over the shit holes."

At the opening dinner, the local oil ministry chairman stood up at the head table and, taut-faced, delivered an unequivocal message in Mandarin to our team that concluded, "We welcome your advice but mostly we subscribe to self-reliance"—a patent rejection at the local level of cooperative venturing with foreign oil companies.

Jiangsu was refusing to accept the dictum of openness to business with the West handed down by the center — an important discovery later shared with our subsidiaries and with the CIA.

At noon the next day, when we broke for lunch and rest, I took a solo trip down the main road. This time, as I entered the wooded area, I realized that I was in the middle of a people's commune. I also observed a small kiosk that sold wines. They might not mix well with Peabody's Coca-Cola, but he probably wouldn't know the difference. Coming onto the road again, I heard the noise of kids playing and noticed an open gate to a schoolyard, one of the elite middle schools (like our prep schools) with which I had become familiar years ago in my doctoral research.

I had almost an hour to kill before the seminar resumed. I just couldn't resist entering the schoolyard, one step at a time. A sweeping glance revealed children of all ages adorned with the red kerchiefs of the Pioneers. They were doing what kids all over do at recess to exercise and have fun: playing sports, chasing each other in made-up games, or enjoying the sliding pond and seesaw. I could see that a whole wing consisted of dormitories. In a far corner of the yard, on a hard dirt area, teenagers were being drilled by one or two slightly older directors in marching and exercise.

Suddenly, as if on cue, every contingent of kids swooped down on me. The older ones, against orders, broke their formation and charged down the incline. Feeling as important as Michael Jackson, I fielded questions in Chinese, debated, and entertained. A young male teacher ultimately came down, and the group parted for him. Smiling and welcoming me, he brought me up to the school office building, which had rows of windows protected with bars on both sides. I told him of my interest in China's young people and their "social" activity. In turn, he invited me to come the next day and speak to his advanced, university-preparatory English language class. His face reddened as a mob of curious children climbed on the windows and roof, many hanging upside down from the eaves to stare into the room.

"The students in my special English class are very mature and preparing for their university examinations," he assured me. I liked the idea of promoting "people-to-people" relations. I suggested that I might bring a couple of "oil patch" buddies whose regional accents varied from the mainstream.

When I returned to our quarters, the oilfield seminar was already in session. Afterwards, stopping at my room, I noticed a gift package on my bed of assorted jars of pickles. It was a present from the school. The peasants seemed to pickle every vegetable and some fruits. There were things in jars that I couldn't recognize. A card in the package welcomed me, thanked me for visiting, and invited me to visit "later" with the principal and chairman of the People's Commune.

Assuming that I was expected, I proposed to visit the principal after our dinner. When the others, Peabody included, argued that 9:00 p.m. was too late for such a personal call, I rationalized that he was drunk and in no condition to render a judgment. But in truth, it was I who was too drunk on Chinese wine and vodka to make any decisions. Peabody frowned and shook his head as I went out the door and wobbled down the dark road to the school, occasionally kicking a divot or two from the packed dirt.

The school gate looked suddenly foreboding, with two stone pillars topped with lamps and the shadow of a uniformed guard. When the guard stepped out of the darkness to confront me, I explained where I was going. He hesitated and then pointed me up the slope. The friendly teacher who had sent the pickles intercepted me.

"We didn't know you'd be coming this late," he said smiling. "But let me escort you to the principal's quarters. He wanted to greet you."

"Maybe it's too late?" I remarked belatedly.

"No, no," and he pulled me in the door to a small three-room apartment adjoining the regular classroom building. Seated in the parlor, the sixty-something principal in pajamas lifted himself uneasily from a soft couch and offered me tea or the Chinese wine he himself had in hand. Foolishly, I chose the wine, and his wife brought a bottle in without saying a word. He didn't get up to turn off the small-screen, black-and-white console TV. As he told me his story, mainly about how he had lost his position and suffered during the Cultural Revolution a decade or more earlier, his wife eyed us warily. As I asked questions and volunteered information about myself, he divided his attention between me and the television and rose again only to turn up the volume on his set. A stand-up comedian now commanded his attention, and he invited me to enjoy the humor with him. I understood only some of the entertainer's fast, Henny Youngman–like gags. I was surprised to learn that the aged comic had been a pre-revolutionary literary figure during the May Fourth Movement, the cultural and nationalistic student movement in the 1920s. Mao Dun was one of the authors I had read in Chinese literature class. Now, his stage act was made up of quips and puns about Mao and the Maoists.

Once again, I made a serious error in judgment. I offered my own would-be humor about Mao and the Cultural Revolution, less like Mao Dun than Woody Allen. Judging from the faces in the room, I bombed. One of them might have tried to feign a laugh but instead choked on his saliva. Trying to redeem my effort to be clever, I faced the principal and grinned: "Don't you think the current 'Four Modernizations' could be just another political movement?"

The principal and teacher cleared their throats in unison. The wife, lurking in the kitchen, poked her head through the doorway with a suspicious scowl, like an illustration of a bitter, servile woman in a Dickensian novel. As her husband was drawn into the discussion, I half-noticed that she scurried across the parlor out the front door.

Bleary-eyed, I took my leave and the teacher invited me to come with the others the next day at noon. "Oh," I said, "I think I've outworn your hospitality."

"No, it would be good," he said.

"Okay, I'll ask a couple of the others, and thanks again." I nodded to the principal, who exuded little emotion. "Thank you for the pickles."

"Will you eat the pickles?" the younger English instructor asked.

"I always have *paocai* with a Chinese meal," I said. "In the States they don't always serve it."

"Oh, *paocai* is quite a bit different, but it's a start," he said.

I stumbled down the hill, past the sentry and back up the road to our dorm, where Peabody gave me a reproving look that was unlike him. The party was breaking up. The next day, after I'd brought the Enserch men over to the school to share their accents with the class in Senior English, we flew to Nanjing and a day later, back to Beijing, where we were to stay at the dismally socialist realist Beijing Hotel.

Feeling good about my encounters in Shaobo, I had entirely forgotten what I had read before the trip in the *People's Daily* about a political movement in China against "sugar-coated bullets" from the West. The Chinese government had clamped down on contamination, particularly of young people, by foreign styles and bourgeois ideas. I didn't even notice my own group's concern that I had seriously overstepped boundaries with the locals. I was shocked when Peabody pulled me aside before we left Nanjing to tell me that I would likely be apprehended, possibly arrested, when we got to Beijing. The charge against me would be "breaking and entering" a middle school. "The group will stick with you," Peabody said quietly in my ear, but an unfamiliar distance now existed between us, and I stood paralyzed.

When we arrived at the airport in Beijing, we all

followed a single line through clearance. Suddenly, an airport employee separated me from the line and took me aside. As the line moved forward, Peabody called, "Don't worry, we're here." But it was clear that they were moving out, and I was being escorted to a screened-off desk behind which sat uniformed police officers.

"Your passport," one policeman demanded. "I will keep it until these matters are fully resolved."

Taken aback by all this foreboding activity, I reassured myself by focusing on the decorous uniforms. We were still very much in the open, and I guessed any more serious plainclothes questioning would take place behind closed doors.

"But it was hardly 'breaking and entering' in any sort of literal sense," I pleaded. Of course, I knew that this phrase could be just a metaphor for my being in the wrong place at the wrong time, a lone individual on a visit that was unscheduled and unprepared.

"Never mind about that now. Your Mr. Chan has assured us that you have been very lonely and homesick. He recommended that rather than restrain you, we should allow you to go back to your wife. Hence, you have been ticketed on the next plane across the Pacific tomorrow. You will fly to Tokyo on the JAL flight. Do you agree?"

I stood in place, stunned. This was the first time I had been tossed out of a country — and it was China.

"We will return your travel documents to Mr. Chan before long. In the meantime, you may pick up your bags ahead and take them through inspection."

I hurriedly ran ahead to grab my luggage and could feel the extra weight of the pickle jars (I loved my souvenirs), wrapped in underwear for safekeeping.

I was ordered to get into a car waiting for me at curbside. This time, I would be traveling in isolation and had no idea where I would be heading. To my relief, we eventually pulled up in front of the hotel, and I was told to return to my room. I was surprised to find that the Texas hands from the "oil patch" behaved discreetly, only seeking to clarify what had happened in hushed voices. I emptied my wallet of scraps of paper with the addresses of the "new friends" that I had made along the way (with special attention to the kids), and Peabody helped me burn them in a dish. Clary offered to carry on his person an English primer that the teacher at the middle school had given me. (I had been privately intrigued by the anti-American epithets and aspersions that had been incorporated into the syntax and grammar examples of the text.) Group leader Peabody carried the remainder of my books and materials. I was ready for my "voluntary deportation."

The guys rode with me to the airport, where I was handed my passport and delivered to the waiting area to board a JAL plane first class. I had to step out to put my bags through security. As I opened the bigger one, one of the inspectors said, "You like pickles?"

"A gift from Chinese frien..." I began to say. Then we all saw the mess—at least two broken jars seeping though my clothes. "Why did I take more than one?" I asked myself.

I was under instructions from the Dallas bosses to fly from Tokyo on the next plane to Hong Kong, where I would stay until the delegation came out of China. Oblivious of time, I phoned my boss when I got to Tokyo's Haneda Airport. He lived in the Washington area, and I got him out of bed. "Do as they say," he said. "But in case you're in Hong Kong for a while, don't overspend."

In the mainland peninsula part of Hong Kong, I found myself a modest room in the rear part of the Peninsula Hotel's old wing, next to an octogenarian friend from an earlier academic trip. He had been the manager for the Sassoons in Shanghai for years before the Second World War, and he lived in their hotel free. It was he who made the arrangement for me with the hotel manager. And I waited—nervous about my job and my whole future in the China field.

Needing to tell my story to someone, I contacted the U.S. Consulate General and ended up baring my soul to two officers from the CIA. They told me that I should have quoted Deng Xiaoping's prescription for an empirical investigation to arrive at the "truth."

I felt anesthetized, drifting, sucked under by an irresistible current. I might as well just let go of all constraints and inhibitions. The future for me was a miasma. I was having a sort of hypermanic episode as a way of dealing with anxiety. I was giddy. I ate, drank, engaged interesting people in the Peninsula lobby tea area who had lived as colonials before war and revolution, and picked up a willowy, green-eyed young woman from the U.S., a tourist who slept with me between her fittings. I ate and drank still more and even agreed to have a late night drink with a young American Chinese female, a student from the research center where I had once worked. Her loose, pear-like breasts bounced against her cut-off shirt as she protested against my insistence that I already was fully committed socially. By this time, I was satisfied with sleeping with the first woman I had met in the lobby.

I stood in the hotel entrance to take a deep breath of air as if it were my last. The noxious aromas of the "fragrant" colony seemed like perfume wafting from the harbor. After so many years of study, I had been asked to leave China. As far I could tell, on the basis of my advice, Enserch Corporation had soured on pursuing any deals there. And all I had for my adventures on the side was a dose of disillusionment and one surviving bottle of pickles.

I'm getting to know the family members at one of the Sichuan drilling sites.

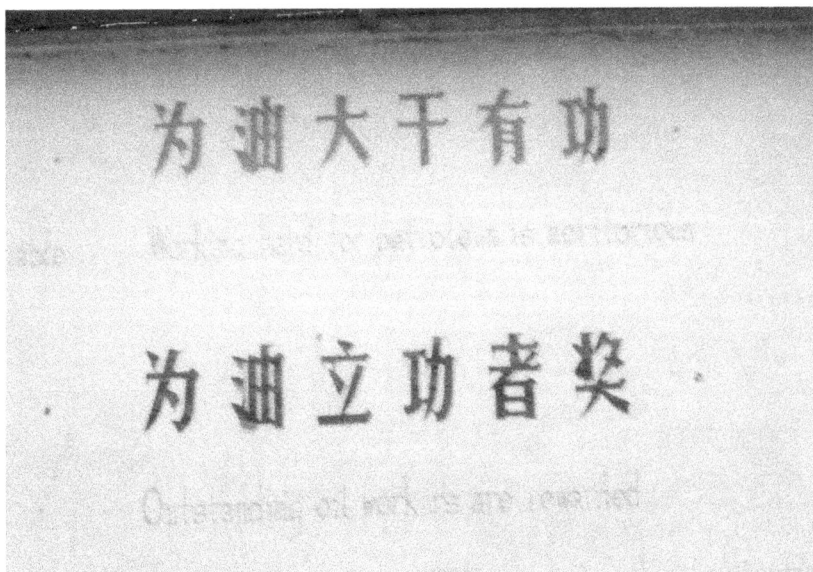

为油大干有功

为油立功者奖

Morale boosting sign to urge petroleum workers forward

The Sichuan oilfield area seems to resemble the U.S. southwest.

The residents, mostly the curious younger generation, come to meet us at the Sichuan field.

The ENSERCH team in Sichuan.

I pose for camera as one of our handlers guesses my age then as over fifty

The main road in Shaobo, Jiangsu, the one where we all took a stroll, and I found the school.

The famous old "Western Theater" on Nanjing Road for screening movies from the West. Some yards away stands the Shanghai Academy of Social Science, where I interviewed young people in 1995.

On 1996 delegation with American conservatives – at the Great Wall.

CHAPTER FOUR

1994

CHINA HOLIDAY

Nearly fifteen years had passed since the Chinese oil ministry (possibly in collusion with Mr. Chan, who saw me as a debunker of his illusions) had asked me to leave China because "my wife was lonely for me, the authorities concluded." At first I was afraid that the China episode in my life might be at an end, but my former professor Michel Oksenberg, then the National Security Council's China advisor, reassured me that I had staying power. He suggested that I try not to forget that my role now was that of a businessman.

I remained at Enserch until the late 1980s, when the conglomerate began to divest itself of its international acquisitions. Post-Enserch, I did some work with Indonesia and served as public affairs adviser to several third-world leaders who had been at loggerheads politically with the United States. Countries like Sandinista-led Nicaragua and Venezuela discovered that they could benefit financially from manipulating the right elites in this country. Consumed with helping the leaders target the most useful individuals and elite groups, I had less time to keep up with my China study. But China was still an intellectual pastime for me, and, after all these years, it seemed like an interesting place to take a holiday.

I did wonder if I were *persona non grata*, but China was big and complex. To my knowledge, the Chinese government's industrial apparatus didn't cough up my name from its computers with a black mark next to it. The ministries and other state organs were so compartmentalized that my visas for a holiday in China with my wife came through quickly. Interestingly, I was issued the documents not through the normal channel of China Travel but through the artifice of an invitation from China Youth Travel. It was 1994, and my wife and I had been approved for unescorted travel, not attached to a group nor assigned to the protective custody of a guide.

As my wife was straightening our clothes for packing, I strutted about expansively, contemplating the grandeur of our trip aloud.

"Annette, I'm taking you to see *my* China."

"Why is it yours?" she responded. "This guesthouse we're staying at, for example—your own friends warned us it was a long way from the center of Beijing and mostly used for delegations."

"Yes, but our oil delegation came back and forth in a motorcade as guests of a state ministry. The splendor and feeling of importance—didn't I tell you how we were treated? A separate chef, the best banquet-style meals— esoteric foods shaped like roosters, marinated jellyfish forming part of a landscape on the table."

"I don't care. The travel agent was going to book us into a luxurious new hotel right near Tiananmen. It would be so much easier to get around than to be in the seclusion of a suburb of Beijing."

"I just want to show you what my first exposure to China was like at its best. You know the grounds are so big there that I got lost."

"You don't expect it to be the same as when your company put up millions and you were the guests of the state, do you?"

"Maybe not. But that in itself might be a story. Relax."

"How could I be expected to remember that the Diaoyutai State Guest House was so far from the airport?" I said, as we rode in a minicab with our bags on our lap to the stately guesthouse.

"I told you that the travel agent and the National Committee for U.S.-China Relations people all said it was unnecessarily far from the center of things."

"How was I to know it was so far? By the way, you know I have a lousy sense of direction, but I think we just passed the stadium site again. Honey, we're really being taken for a ride. It feels like being on the D.C. Beltway."

I shouted in the direction of the cab driver, "I'll tell you again in 'ordinary language' (national language)," We want to go to Diaoyutai Guest House, sir." I leaned forward and threw my upper body over the back of the front seat.

"Oh? You mean *Guobingyuan* (state guesthouse)," the cabbie responded. "Sorry, must turn around," he said in bad English.

I turned to Annette. "It's like being a 'rube' in New York. *Ni pian women!* (You're cheating us)," I yelled at the driver.

"No, no," he said without turning his head.

Annette, fighting jetlag, wasn't quite centered during this first episode in Beijing. I had experienced every possible variation of "I told you so" by the time we arrived. When we did face the formidable gate, we pulled up to a cul-de-sac where the cab could be checked before being admitted. The bayonet-bearing guards gave the vehicle the once-over, less to search it than to project, *"Where did you get this heap, and how can you have face coming here in it? And to top it all off, you want us to open the gates for just one car and not a train of vehicles?"*

I registered with a person who meandered from the back of what looked like a ticket kiosk in front. Outer perimeter reception, I imagined. I was surprised at the frowns and sneers. The employees didn't seem to enjoy working at what was now, at least temporarily, a tourist hotel. The cab wasn't permitted to enter. I pulled out a wad of dollars to pay the driver and gasped when I saw the meter. Not since a taxi in Rome had taken me to another town instead of to a downtown Chinese restaurant had I been so ripped off. I started to count out the money after reminding him that he had gone around in circles, and the driver just held out his hand indifferently. My rage reached the tips of my fingers, and I dumped the rest of the small change all over the vehicle and the pavement. "Your tip!" I said. I knew that in any case, I hadn't even paid the fare that he sought. He tentatively stooped to pick up the coins and few bills.

"I am Chinese, one of the *people*," he pleaded to the military guard standing over us.

I explained to the officer how he had taken advantage of me, "…And furthermore, I speak Chinese," I added.

The officer lunged with his bayonet, striking a pose between the two of us as if in a revolutionary ballet. In turn, the other soldiers in phalanx formation in the rear moved forward with their bayonets extended. The cab driver jumped into his cab. I stood motionless. "Go!" snapped the officer at us and gestured toward the gates as they opened.

Annette said, "I told you we'd be better off downtown." We dragged our bags inside the gate until intercepted by a makeshift bellboy.

Our room reminded me a little of other tourist facilities with a socialist realist decor. We were advised that we could keep our door open all the time. Dinner was served in a small room on a balcony overlooking a lavish ballroom still in need of cleaning from an earlier party. That evening for dinner we ate something that seemed to be a replica of an arcane traditional dish of quail's eggs and a small dish of tiny dumplings, the apparent leftovers from the party downstairs. We both went to bed hungry, hoping that in the morning we could get some normal eggs at least. Neither of us had much to say to the other.

We awoke to a nice breakfast that turned out to be a sendoff. The young man who had carried our bags told us that they needed the room back for a delegation ("You were once here with a delegation, and you came now just for nostalgia's sake?" he asked). The cleaning woman growled some words that I was unable to distinguish. The luggage man, apparently also the hotelier, had booked a hotel for us downtown—the very hotel that we would have chosen in the first place. And he called a "proper" sedan from China Travel Service to whisk us away.

The Wangfuzi Hotel was so nice that it made me seem an utter fool for considering something so out of the way and just as expensive. The next day, the same car took us to the Ming Tombs, the Great Wall, and Tiananmen and the Forbidden City (a palace complex hitherto forbidden to us by its distance from the guesthouse). We were now well on our way to treating this sojourn as a holiday.

Our mood was marred, however, by the fact that I spoke the national Chinese language (the dialect spoken well and clearly by Beijing natives), while Annette knew only a few words learned in Hong Kong more than two decades earlier. Naturally, she expected me to be her translator. But as my Chinese improved and I became more confident, I often got caught up in a lengthy discourse with the driver, a child on the street, a tourist from another part of China, and others. Annette felt excluded from our laughter and shared thoughts, and when I finally made an effort to interpret, I reduced every exchange to a bare minimum; I was having too good a time with my Chinese companions. I was a little like Bill Murray's director in the movie *Lost in Translation*, impatient with Annette's queries in English and her interruptions. Ultimately, she saw Beijing as a foreign film without subtitles and missed all its liveliness and personality, and I in turn experienced her bitterness.

In Shanghai, it was my turn to have trouble communicating in the local dialect. "Ordinary Chinese" (the national language) would usually work, but I was like an outsider from some other place communicating in a common second language. It wasn't the same as speaking Shanghainese. Except for the semi-colonial waterfront with its early twentieth century skyscrapers, Shanghai to me was just another big city, the world's biggest Chinatown.

My major piece of serious business was to track down some of the so-called avant-garde artists who had cropped up in the mid to late 1980s. I knew that many of the renegades from traditional techniques in painting had come through the graphics institutes scattered around, in Beijing, Shanghai, Hangzhou, Sichuan, and elsewhere.

We had planned to visit the graphics institute in Shanghai because the city's size gave us good odds of making some contacts. Although I had called ahead to the school's administration, the gatekeeper wasn't expecting us. I explained that we did have an appointment. Before long, a teacher emerged to show us to a current exhibition of faculty and student works. I have never seen coached works that were so imitative and banal. We didn't stay long and emerged, disappointed, onto a grassy stretch leading to bicycle racks.

Our escort from the institute pointed to a man just arriving on a bicycle and urged us to talk with him, one of their leading artists. He was pleasant and was (conveniently) able to show us a catalog of his sculpture—mostly public monuments celebrating heroes of war and revolution. When he suggested that we accompany him to see his studio, we found ourselves hesitating and making excuses.

Suddenly, I felt someone grab me from behind and say, "You want to see some abstract and modern art? Come with me." A longhaired, slightly disheveled fellow in his late thirties said, "I'm Sun Liang. I'll take you to see my work first, and then I can introduce you to Ding Yi and other artists like me. I graduated from this school, but you won't find anything here."

We all got in a cab, and I excitedly began to take notes for a series of articles that would appear in print over the next couple of years.

Toward the end of our stay in Shanghai, I was feeling so buoyantly excited about the prospect of writing articles on the avant-garde movement in the arts that I began to think even bigger. Why not make a return to the China field by adapting my interviewing techniques to this generation of Chinese youth in Shanghai? I already had done some recent interviewing at Columbia. And at Princeton, working within a program of acculturation for young activists rescued from Tiananmen Square in 1989, I helped the youth who voluntarily came to me to recall the events and the emotions that motivated them. I wondered how I might arrange for a grant to undertake some serious research in the China field, gathering material possibly suitable for a trade book.

Looking out the window of our room at the Shanghai Hilton, I suddenly recalled that an old China scholar from my days as an undergraduate at Cornell had returned to China and had become president of the Shanghai Academy of Social Sciences, a nongovernmental think-tank around the corner. I wondered whether he was still alive. With only two days remaining in Shanghai, calling on him "cold" would be a long shot.

Dr. Zhang Zhong-li, ironically the author of a book called *The Chinese Gentry* (University of Washington Press), turned out to be a member of the government elite nationally and in Shanghai. My spur-of-the-moment phone call from the hotel room set off a flurry of calls, and eventually I got through to Zhang Zhong-li, who invited me to lunch at the Academy. Another call from a fellow who identified himself as the chief of the Academy's Department of International Affairs explained the precise arrangements: I was to meet privately now with Dr. Zhang. My wife would remain in our hotel room until the chief phoned her to meet him in the lobby, whence he would escort her to join us for lunch.

Zhang, whom I had never met, had been an able scholar. I complimented his book on the prerevolutionary gentry, and he seemed intrigued by my work on successive post-revolutionary generations of youth. While we talked and I sank deeper into my cushy armchair, the International Affairs officer, who looked younger but might have been approaching thirty, was interrogating Annette en route. The ride should have been short; he must have gone a few streets out of his way or else spoken quickly. He asked about her career and background, and seemed pleased to find that she was a professional social worker who had devoted her energies to working with people of color in a New York City housing project. Then he gradually moved the discussion to my background. I had studied in Taiwan. Did I favor Taiwan? Did I still have friends from Taiwan? Why was I drawn to China as a subject of interest? Did I like China?

A few relevant members of the Academy were already seated around a table in a modest-looking restaurant adjoining the Academy when Zhang and I entered, and my wife and her escort joined us. Zhang had been having a hard time ordering the meal, as the kitchen had few of the dishes listed on the menu. The repast unfolded slowly, so we had a long time for serious discussion of my work and what I would like to do in Shanghai the following year. The consensus was that, after some paperwork, I would be approved for next year's academic calendar. I would fund the travel and research. We lifted our beers and toasted the relationship.

The main course consisted of stale shrimp that had died in the tank before being cooked. I noticed that Professor Zhang wouldn't eat his, perhaps because they had the consistency of mashed potatoes. "There's twice-cooked pork," he said. "I am used to that." "And we have twice-dead shrimp today."

CHAPTER FIVE

1995

I CAN GIVE IT IN CHINESE

It was late at night, and I was tired and disoriented and wasn't even sure this was the right place. It was a rundown residential hotel, an ironic monument to the signing of the Communiqué between Zhou Enlai and Kissinger in 1972. Now, some more than twenty years later, I was about to step out into a parking lot with a small Chinese man peering through the rear window. He was there to greet me. But he hadn't troubled to meet me at the airport, nor did he waste much time on polite talk. He declared, "We'll want you to give a presentation on your research, from the Cultural Revolution to the insights you have for us since Tiananmen."

"Sure, I can give it in Chinese," I answered without hesitation.

I was feeling grandiose about the prospect of telling Chinese experts on youth, education, and social control about my impressions of the collective psyche of the generations of teenagers in post-revolutionary China. Mr. Chen, who was to be my academic unit head at the Shanghai Academy of Social Sciences, said, "In Chinese, no less? Can you do it?" It was 1995, almost thirty-five years since my last class or tutorial in the language. He wouldn't tell me then or afterward that my Mandarin

Chinese was almost as convoluted as his own (he was used to speaking Shanghai dialect most of the time). Chen probably thought, "Let the guy sink or swim. If he looks foolish, it can't hurt us." He didn't seem to like working with foreign scholars. His younger, more scholarly associate, perhaps detecting the self-doubt leaking through the cracks in my ego, said, grinning, "How would we Shanghainese know whether you pronounce the national language correctly?" A thirty-something man, gaunt with sallow cheeks, "Tall Yang" had a gentler demeanor and paleness that that made him look frail. He seemed more sensitive.

Chen was the head of the Youth Affairs department; he tended to administrative matters and his associate handled the academic output and supervision. "Youth" was no more curious a line of multidisciplinary study than Holocaust Studies in our universities. When I arrived at this "liberal" think-tank (theoretically in the private sector), I had higher expectations than to be working under Mr. Chen, who looked more like a handler or Communist Party runner than an intellectual. Slightly stoop-shouldered, with a full, smoke-stained smile, he lacked the proud bearing of the "traditional" Chinese scholars whom I had met in Taiwan or at the American universities where I had studied.

Now, in China proper, in my forties, instead of a encountering a collegial or comradely reception, I was under the supervision of a cold bureaucrat, already feeling an oppression that was characteristic of the whole Chinese social environment. Chen cared more for business and obeisance than books or manners. One suitcase still in hand and weighing on my arm, I listened to his demands for an advance on my expenses. I abruptly reminded him that I had made a financial commitment and would honor it *after* I had recovered from jetlag.

Scrutinizing me with all the trust of a border guard, he announced that even though it was late in the day, he wanted to go over my interviewing agenda. I had proposed that impressionistic, psychological interviewing of young Chinese might give me some sort of fix on personality types in the post-Tiananmen massacre generation. The rapport-building technique was critical to my work on Chinese adolescents and their relation to authority. As an American anthropologist friend put it, "How could they let you do such subversive stuff?" But in negotiations with the Academy director, and in subsequent correspondence, this think-tank had seemed to see nothing threatening in my social scientific snooping.

As I sat on the edge of my bed, I had to listen to this administrative type recite schedule changes for youngsters I'd yet to meet. It was late in the evening, and I just wanted to close my eyes, but I needed to get one thing straight. "You never indicated whether I could sit alone with each kid and pursue the lines of questioning that I indicated in letters to you."

"You see," Chen began as he looked past me. "Last minute, the International Affairs [Security] department of the Academy wanted to disinvite you over concern that you might touch on too many compromising areas. But I thought no, it would be a loss of face."

"Loss of whose face?" I wondered. This curtain-raiser

was foreboding. I already had enough concerns about my ability to interview in private and establish a personal rapport with young people, given my limited time in Shanghai. Even with interviews bugged, I had hoped that these adolescents would be inured to what they couldn't see. They would be apt to react in a much more inhibited way to one or two authoritative Chinese adults cocking their heads and maybe even calling the signals from just a few feet away.

"According to my method, there should be only interviewer and interviewee in the room. I have to create a psychological rapport and try to bond..."

I tried to conceal my anguish with an agreeable smile, but maybe Chen read something else into it. He suddenly seemed to rear back, muttering, "You should be grateful that we let you come. Perhaps you look down on Tall Yang and me. Tall Yang has only a master's, but that is the equivalent of a Ph.D. and means even more in China."

"Oh, no, you misunderstand," I said. "It's just that I don't see how I can work without circumstances of confidentiality and trust."

"Yes, we'll try to maintain quiet. Just that Mr. Yang and I will stand off to the side in case you need help with your Chinese. And these kids can be so shy, too."

"Oh..." I moaned to myself. "I might as well spend the rest of my time in China sightseeing."

My first day in the office was filled with uncertainty and ups and down. Though the Chinese adolescents were a mixture of sexes, personalities, and ages, they were all attractive — hardly a random sample, but picked by Tall

Yang after proper vetting. They blended so well that they would have been better suited to some version of the Mickey Mouse Club. Had there been auditions? This was not a place to look for spontaneity and openness.

Arranging the room, a former cloakroom for receptions in the conference room next door, I moved a schoolteacher's desk toward the far wall. The interviewee and I would sit in metal armchairs, facing one another close to the center of the room. A spare wooden chair, I pushed to the far corner. The room was cluttered but windowless and Spartan. A narrow door behind me connected with the large seminar room.

I was surprised when, even before the first session had run its course, Mr. Chen, apparently finding the exchange too slow or boring, got off the desk and left the room. Mr. Yang held the fort. He intervened once to try to goad a kid who seemed to be afraid to tell me something in particular about his childhood. I stopped him. A bit later he attempted to clarify my Chinese to a youngster. Ultimately, he too seemed to have fulfilled an obligation and quietly stole out of the room. In my self-centeredness, at the time I took this to be a personal triumph—it wasn't. Decorum for the most part stood the test and the mood had been set. The concealed listening devices would do their job.

Most of the interviews were stilted. And when one precocious middle-schooler let the words flow like lava, I squirmed in my chair at the thought that this might be a put-up job. The next schoolchild, a grinning little girl aged twelve, turned out to be the editor-in-chief of the *Shanghai Children's Newspaper*.

In an effort to quell my despair, a Chinese artist friend from an earlier trip offered to let me interview some young friends in his studio. But it soon became clear that he had a second occupation with public security. I made up my mind to relax a bit and go with the flow.

I wasn't able to probe very deeply given the limitations of the pool of interviewees and my short time in China. The interviewing wound down when one of the younger, inexperienced kids got scared in the wake of a meeting with me and told his teacher that I had mentioned the 1989 "Tiananmen" clash. "Politics is a no-no," admonished Chen. In the few days following, I was told to taper off and prepare my speech for the invitational seminar in the conference room next door. The subject would be the psychological dimension of the political behavior of Chinese youth, from the Cultural Revolution to the present. "Politics," it seemed, was a subject forbidden as a subject of discourse; for debriefings, it was mandatory.

The last interviews at the Shanghai Academy were difficult to conduct because of the hammering and ripping of the construction work underway in the sedately furnished, lounge-like facility next door. One morning, I even found torn lumber and nails jutting into the adjoining doorway of my office. I peered into the conference room for the first time since the din had begun and observed many of the red plush armchairs removed or pushed into a semicircle at the front of the chamber. Clumsy wooden chairs, thick wires, and debris were scattered toward the rear. I was afraid to ask why the seminar room was apparently being remodeled.

On the eve of my talk, I had nervously crafted a rough

script in Chinese. In recent days, I had made new friends at the U.S. Consulate General in Shanghai, and one or two foreign men asked to join me at my table in the hotel dining room. A really nice older gentleman was almost like a therapist in his reassuring conversation about my activities. He later told me that he had been a colonel in the Special Forces in Vietnam, and handed me a business card with a Nob Hill, San Francisco address. Another man whom I had taken for just a bureaucrat at the U.S. Consulate took me aside to give me a thorough briefing on Deng Xiaoping's state of health and general concerns about the liberalism of potential successors. And all of them—in one way or another—suggested that my talk might be reaching Prime Minister Li Peng, the very man who had ordered the tanks into Tiananmen Square six years earlier. In my recent work, I had renounced this sort of repressive authoritarianism at the top of the system and noted that its persistence over time could affect the child-rearing practices of those scions who had been brought up more permissively. They would cognitively want to teach their children to be conscious of properly deferential behavior. Moreover, the 'put downs' that they experienced now in the workplace would find their way back into the home environment.

On the day of the presentation, I got to the conference room early and peered into the lounge as the invited guests gathered. Mr. Chen grabbed me, pulled me into his office, and had me sum up my talk quickly. He nodded his approval. Returning to the conference forum, I felt that I was staring at a stage set. I noted that the older 1950s generation of cadres seemed to occupy the few plush armchairs in front. A battery of floodlights and spots shone on the front of the room and on the lectern where I would be positioned. I had never participated in a seminar that was so formal and staged.

While there was time, I crept over to the lectern just to get the feel. Casting a glance toward the rear of the room, I noticed a lens protruding slightly from the innards of the back wall. Numb now and concerned that I hadn't adequately prepared for a major address rather than an informal talk, I slinked out of the room.

My God, I had stage fright. Minutes seemed like hours till Mr. Chen summoned me into the room. The glare of the lights was so strong I could barely see the people seated on the folding wooden chairs in the back. Most of them seemed to be middle-aged, or perhaps a bit younger. Mr. Chen introduced me to the audience as Tall Yang smiled benignly from his corner red armchair. I looked at my notes (mostly in Chinese), and I was so paralyzed for a minute that my own Chinese characters no longer made sense to me.

I greeted the audience in perfect Mandarin to a sea of smiles. These soon faded into many twisted facial expressions as the scholars in the room tried to grasp what I was saying. The whirring of a camera from the back wall of the room was a real distraction. Adlibbing in Chinese, I expressed simple ideas in complex Chinese and tough psychological concepts, like "introjected father," in words that were too simple.

Having given them the gist of my approach and my findings, I threw the session open to Q. and A. Questions mostly emanated from the rear. One woman criticized the language I had used to describe opposing one's father, an expression I had intended as a deliberate overstatement in archaic, Maoist revolutionary language. Another person, waving her hand in the very rear (I saw her easily because the intense lights had been lowered), asked me what I thought of the Chinese exchange students whom I had interviewed in the States.

"Most seemed to be what we would call 'spoiled'— perhaps because of the one-child law," I replied. "They tended to be narcissistic, self-centered, and very 'bourgeois,' maybe because of the U.S. environment." I saw people squirm a bit in their chairs (even the soft ones). U.S.-Chinese educational exchanges had reached a new peak that year, and so-called liberals at the Party center were still contending with the old-guard Communists over foreign contamination.

"What do you propose we do about the problem?" the fortyish woman asked, leaning forward, a sardonic smile feeling its way across the curl in her lips.

I paused and smiled sheepishly. "You might consider sending fewer kids to the United States."

She pushed away her chair, as if she were about to bolt from the room. Then she seated herself again and assumed a poker face. Chortles seemed to issue from the front orchestra, creating a ripple effect that swept through the bridge chairs all the way in back. Yang, the friendly young associate on the edge of the row of plush seats, couldn't restrain his laughter.

At a sign from Mr. Chen, I summed up my thoughts

about the potential for rebelliousness once a youth acceded to a work role. The adult society, I said, would discourage the individual from earlier-learned individualistic inclinations or confrontation with authority. The applause that followed was respectful, even if not really enthusiastic. But I took comfort in the few older generation cadres who approached me smiling and apparently interested in making conversation. (I did have fans after all.)

I made my way back to my interviewing office, which now looked more like the cloakroom it was meant to be. Tall Yang entered, smiled wanly, and told me to wait. In what seemed like several minutes, the junior member of the department, a girl not yet twenty-three, appeared in the doorway. I had met this young woman at perhaps two departmental meals. She swept in like a plotting courtesan in a Peking opera. I stood alone waiting for a handshake. "You were incomprehensible. No one understood your ideas. You failed!"

"Maybe they're better off," I said, trying to make light of her patently harsh comment. I wondered whether I was wrong about confrontation being considered less appropriate in this post-Maoist era. "Don't you know how to be respectful, young lady?"

"You asked for our thoughts," she said.

"But not necessarily expressed without tact," I said. I didn't expect to be criticized as if I were a "class enemy." She grinned slightly. "A little of the non-antagonistic, 'fine drizzle' criticism would be better for a guest."

I thought to myself that she might well have come from

a type of home socialization where rebellion, particularly among daughters, takes the form of violent defiance of elders. (Too bad that I couldn't have interviewed her about her childhood.) She brought me back to the Cultural Revolution period: the piercing sounds in deafening bleats, the voices of teenage daughters trying to bring down the walls of Jericho and raise Mao even higher, the defiant shouts of Jiang Qing (Mao's widow and the leader of the 'Gang of Four') as she stood trial for her abuses of power against the people.

"I'm not interested in talking any further," I said and strode back into the nearly empty conference room.

"But I speak for the group!" she called after me.

By this time, my friend the colonel, who had first followed me to the hotel restaurant, had changed his room to the one facing mine. Lingering in China for the avowed purpose of management consulting (he always carried a light attaché case), he used "just enough Chinese language" to be polite. He pronounced the words with an accentuated Texas drawl. After hours of conversation, I was fairly certain that he was a CIA operative.

He sat with me at our usual table where we could talk seriously or comment on the young waitresses. "Congratulations," he said. "You did fine, right?"

"By the way, it *was* Li Peng," he said, "on closed circuit."

He nodded with a "Ni hao" to the waitress, who appeared at our table, in a way that combined his Texas drawl with an exaggerated pronunciation of Chinese tones.

I smiled and remarked, "I don't know whether I told them what they wanted to know or needed to know. I should have stuck to English. But it was an experience."

"Any interesting feedback?" the colonel asked.

"No fresh insights," I smiled sourly. "Except that this place becomes increasingly unfriendly and Kafkaesque — and this is hardly my first trip."

"Oh, is that so?" He pushed away slowly from the table, grinned, and said, "By the way, I'll be going inland tomorrow and probably won't be seeing you again. You have my card. Call me when you get back. One of us will be following me here. Watch out for the bad guys, kid."

CHAPTER SIX

NOVEMBER 1996

TALKING THE RIGHT LANGUAGE TO WORK?

In 1996, I returned from my research in Shanghai to try to do some serious writing on the anti-authority behavior of this generation of China's urban youth. I sat in my office and tried to piece together the best of my interview material with specific incidents reported in the Chinese press. And I continued to write to other think-tanks and libraries in China that might accommodate my needs after that test run in Shanghai.

In those days, the U.S. still had some leverage over China. Foreign investment, and the U.S. share in particular, constituted the engine of China's rapid economic growth. As President Clinton prepared for a formal visit to China, Wang Dan, a leading dissident in the Tiananmen democracy movement, was released from prison. He had been interned for plotting to "overthrow the government," an unreasonably harsh conviction carrying a sentence of eleven years. Chinese authorities meant to show respect for President Clinton's imminent visit. Meanwhile, in the U.S., presidential contenders were stumbling to shape campaigns, but both the Dole Republicans and Clinton were deeply committed to continuing to push forward China's modernization (it looked as if the Chinese had contributed heftily to Bill Clinton's campaign).

Columbia's East Asian Institute and Business School invited me to give a presentation at their University Seminar series—my gift to Columbia in return for a visiting position as a research associate there. Members of the faculty were less interested in China's youth (a subject seemingly passé now) than in my expertise as a corporate political risk analyst. The idea of performing in front of my peers and mentors was daunting, but this time the language of my discipline and native country would roll off my tongue. I took a brief break from what I had been doing and prepared a dramatic paper on my approach to risk analysis and its application to the People's Republic of China.

As I took my place at the seminar table, a tall, heavy Chinese man, dripping from the rain outside, took a seat right next to me. With an ingratiating smile, he nodded an apology for interrupting the chair's introduction, which referred to me as a "renaissance man." Extending his hand, he whispered, "Sorry. I'm Joe Wei." Later, describing himself as an editor and writer for the Chinese-language New York newspaper *World Journal* (Da Shijie), Wei asked me to join him for dim sum in Chinatown the next weekend. He and I shared the first of many "gossip" sessions about China. He always seemed to have more of an interest in American China scholars and developments in China than in the cultural and human-interest features actually in his charge at the paper. At one get-together, however, when I talked about the Red Guards whom I had interviewed in 1971-1972 after they escaped to Hong Kong, Joe suggested that I write a piece for his paper on my work with these refugee youth.

"Make it a summary of your interviewing work, and we'll try to find some of these people. You could write later for a magazine on where they are now and how they think now that they are in a more democratic, capitalist environment." It seemed like an interesting idea. I never anticipated that Joe would print my home phone number in the last paragraph of the article.

No one I had known in Hong Kong came forth. Instead, the responses emanated from a variety of readers and others who were told about the article afterward, the largest demographic group being cooks, waiters, and dishwashers at Chinese restaurants who called after work in the wee hours of the morning. For weeks after the story ran, my phone rang at all hours, and not one of those refugees I knew to have been America-bound ever turned up.

Months elapsed. My "infomercial" had failed.

I didn't hear from Joe Wei for some time. I had invited him and his wife to dinner at our Brooklyn brownstone more than once, but he never accepted. "I don't like to involve my family," he later confided elliptically. One afternoon, Joe rang me up. No longer a research associate at Columbia, I had now been out of work for some months. "Are you still looking for a China-related position?" he asked.

"That depends," I said.

"I've got a Washington-based think-tank you would be perfect for. All their policy people will probably go into the Dole Administration."

"Dole?"

"Yeah, I assume that you're a Republican."

"Why?" I protested. "I'm a Democrat. Besides, Bob Dole hasn't even been nominated yet. Where'd you hear about this position?"

"I was at a conference on security issues in Washington," he replied. "And the American Foreign Relations Association's president, Herman Kirschner, asked me if I knew a good China person."

"Joe, you certainly get around for someone who is 'U.S. Features and Sunday Features Editor' in New York."

"I like to pursue my personal interests, David."

"Dole is very conservative," I said, "and I doubt that I'd have much of an influence with his team."

"Why not see what the fit is like?" Joe responded. "I think you could have a good dialogue with them. Talk to Kirschner."

When I did phone Kirschner, after arguing with Annette, relatives, and friends about the feasibility of changing political ideas from within, he recognized my name immediately and seemed receptive, and we set a meeting at the think-tank's headquarters on Massachusetts Ave., NW. Trying to do a bit of preliminary research on the organization, I visited the Foundation Center in lower Manhattan, which, the librarian assured me, had the most comprehensive array of reference materials on not-for-profits in the United States. I stressed that this "foundation" was political and low profile, but she smiled confidently and proceeded to cross-index for any reference to the organization, its annual report, or its funding. We came up empty-handed. My conclusion: Perhaps I was dealing with the CIA or something even more hidden. I was more curious than before to meet Herman Kirschner.

When I got to the Georgetown-style brick building, I entered a wide-open room and scanned the few furnishings. In an eating area that looked like a booth in a diner, I saw photographs on the wall of NSC advisor and former professor Zbigniew Brzezinski (perhaps the lone Democrat) and other familiar public personalities, their "grunts," and their backers.

"Mr. Raddock—Dave!" someone called from the upper landing of a winding staircase. "Our offices are up here."

Winded from my aggressive rush to the top of the stairway, I shook the man's hand.

"Herman Kirschner. Let me show you around."

What a grip, I thought, as his chest pushed against his jacket. "You've got the whole building?" I asked as I tried to discern what concerto was playing loudly on the stereo in his office.

"Goodness, no," he said. "We just have this half of the top floor—or, I should say, landing. That's Brahms. I was just having some tea. Care for some?" I nodded. "We have London breakfast or Earl Grey? Sorry, no Chinese Oolong." He proceeded to tell me about himself and the organization. "We are more diverse than you think," he said, adjusting his thick-lensed glasses. "I'm a neoconservative Republican, but my wife works for the EPA—she would have to be a Democrat," he chuckled. "I used to be an NCAA wrestler at my college in Ohio. Now I'm less interested in competing—athletically, that is.

AFRA is a not-for-profit," he went on. "I'll give you a tour."

"Do you have an annual report or budget for AFRA?" I asked.

"Oh, yes, but the circulation is small. I'd have to look for a copy."

We crossed the landing and found a thirty-something guy working amid all sorts of papers.

Herman introduced us, and we shook hands. "He raised all the grants and what not to fund a democracy-in-the-eastern-bloc journal himself," Kirschner announced, as if to make a particular point.

"Dave, you could sit in this small office on the corner, but the lovely woman from California who arranges all our fundraisers in Orange County comes here to use it maybe two days a week and meets her daughter here from preschool. But you two can work it out. ...Come in my office. I'd like to discuss your thoughts and your salary needs."

I was very articulate that afternoon. I got the job, and I came out the easy winner in negotiations for how much salary I would be paid. As I left, we agreed that I would come again the next week and start to work on raising money for my position. "When would I submit my expenses?" I asked matter-of-factly as I prepared to leave.

"Oh," said Kirschner, "we can't pay expenses yet either. That'll start at the same time we're able to provide your salary. Once you bring in enough money from donors, you'll realize both salary and expenses. I'll have the formal announcements of your appointment made up for you by your next visit. We'll do them very elegantly."

"I'll think about doing some issue papers," I said in partial denial of what he had just said.

"That can wait. We want to attend first to our trip to China. After all, their group was here almost a year ago. We've got to reciprocate and keep the dialogue going!"

Over the next weeks, I followed orders and managed surprisingly to raise some thousands of dollars, which a rich and conservative matron who lived at the Watergate and taught Bible classes at church matched several times over. Soon I would be back in the People's Republic of China on a political mission. Like our big donor, the AFRA delegation would be representing its gospel. But I still would be without pay.

CHAPTER SEVEN

NOVEMBER 1996

MOTORCADE MAELSTROM

On this mission, the Chinese put us up at the Equatorial Hotel, a lodging that had originally been built to honor "third world" visitors of color. The irony struck me immediately.

My biggest financial supporter was a Chinese-American man who had responded to Joe Wei's newspaper article about my work on the Red Guards. Even before he told me his story, George Hu looked like a victim: with his lifelong grief and soft physique, he might have been a school bully's favorite target. He had come from a very rich family and had in fact watched his father beaten by his own Red Guard classmates from junior middle school at the beginning of the Cultural Revolution. With many grievances to redress, George planned to accompany us, hoping to show up our Communist hosts. He supposed, as did I, that the prestigious former National Security Advisor to President Clinton, Zbigniew Brzezinski, would lead the group.

But with U.S. national elections only a week away, few current political personalities of distinction were available for a trip. Then why not let me direct the delegation? Kirschner's answer was that only government figures of note could secure our appointments with the high-level

Chinese officials whose names I had proposed. At our helm, in the event, were a past assistant secretary of state for agriculture under Nixon, now a private consultant, and an assistant secretary of defense from the same era, now an arms dealer.

Our motorcade's first stop from the airport wasn't the hotel but the Ideological Section of the Chinese Communist Party. The woman who spoke formulated a familiar new mix of socialism and privatization and outlined a set of behavioral norms that had been adopted by the standing committee of the Politburo of the Chinese Communist Party. She photocopied the proposed directive and handed the document to me at the conclusion of the meeting. When leaders go to this much trouble to emphasize their ideological credibility, it is because they sense that they will be perceived as weak in that area or not sufficiently legitimate.

For their part, the former assistant secretaries, sitting closest to the host, were bent on reciting a series of trite, hard-line questions about the impact of China's policy on the U.S. and world interests, a script they would repeat from meeting to meeting with an assortment of Chinese officials, including the vice chairman of the National People's Congress. Would China continue to aid North Korea militarily? Did China sell vital nuclear components to Iran? What did the PRC plan to do about redressing the balance of trade between China and the United States? What about the Chinese government's human rights violations? There was something sinister about the way these two men—of no public reputation—intimated that they represented the Republican point of view, pretending to convey the tenor of Reagan's thoughts and hinting at having been anointed by Richard Nixon (during whose administration they had been merely fledgling bureaucrats).

Meanwhile, Kirschner turned and handed me a notepad and pen, implying that he'd heard enough from me. Ironically, after the meeting, the Ideology Section secretary also turned to me to continue some additional thoughts informally. I think she was pleased that she had engaged my attention and enjoyed the friendly exchange.

Tired and cranky, we sought our rooms to freshen ourselves before the opening banquet at the Diaoyutai Guest House, to be hosted by the vice minister for foreign affairs. (The assistant secretaries acted as if our hosts had used the briefing as a device to stall us while the housekeeping staff made the beds.) But while most us languished from jet lag, a reenergized George Hu entertained a private visitor behind a closed door, a politician, Wen Jiabao, who would later become China's premier.

When we gathered near the elevators to join the motorcade, Kirschner, seemingly annoyed with my proactive involvement, thrust another pad into my hands, saying, "We'll need good notes."

"Herman, I really don't think it's appropriate at a formal dinner," I said, smiling. "I can put down my impressions afterward."

"No, you need to take it," he said. "We must have notes." There was no sense wrestling with a wrestler. I carried it with me as unobtrusively as possible.

When we arrived at Diaoyutai (the state guesthouse of which I had so many memories, good and bad) and walked tentatively into the banquet hall. Everyone in the host party was standing at his seat—and everyone except the vice foreign minister, who stood at the head of a large round table, held a notepad and pen in hand as if poised to play a musical instrument. I grinned at this unsubtle diplomatic signal from the Chinese, took my seat next to a young junior officer and placed my writing utensils on the plush green carpet at my side. The others then in unison also dropped theirs. Kirschner looked away.

The tastefully dressed young man at my side, still in his thirties, was a rising star at the Chinese Foreign Ministry's "America Desk." In the course of congenial conversation, I asked some very direct questions. When I asked about the imprisoned democratic dissident Wang Dan, who had received a lot of world press, he reproached me for exploring an inappropriate area. I laughed heartily and said that I thought he should be more open with those of us who respected China. He relented, smiling, and we discussed the matter.

I asked him as well about the need for armed conflict to resolve the Taiwan question. But first I told him that I had long felt that Taiwan should be under the PRC's sovereignty. He smiled agreeably and offered an interpretation—most remarkable for that early time—of how economic and social ties between Taiwan and China would multiply and become so complex that unification would follow *ad hoc*.

The urge to go to the bathroom interrupted my flow of thought. George Hu was also excusing himself for the same purpose. I found him at a urinal and made some small talk about the assistant secretaries as we were relieving ourselves. George nearly sprayed me as he gesticulated wildly toward the ceiling.

"Don't you know there are microphones all around us?" he whispered with panicked, in-the-lair-of-the-enemy urgency. I couldn't tell whether this was an affectation or whether he was genuinely frightened.

"Why are you so guarded?" I asked him. "Relax. You don't have to overreact." I bowed over into my urinal and thanked my hosts for a nice meal. And then I laughed.

George muttered, "You're crazy!"

As we got into our cars, I smilingly offered to return Kirschner's notebook. "Keep it with you," he said, frowning.

The next day was filled with a trip to the Great Wall and with side visits to other tourist spots. In spare moments waiting for our turn to climb the wall as a group, I attempted to brief our people about relevant history at the various sites. I gratuitously threw in some discussion of political movements and the Great Proletarian Cultural Revolution. The former assistant secretary of state for agriculture in particular behaved as if he either knew it all or was determined to shield the group from my version. Instead he changed the subject to a recently published novel about atrocities, *White Swan*, which they had all been reading as "preparation" for the trip.

Our trek up the steps of the Great Wall began, and the assistant secretary for agriculture—at this point the self-proclaimed No. 1 leader of the delegation—lurched ahead screaming that he would make it to the very top. Shortly after, he hurtled down the stone block steps waving a certificate he had bought at the top, which attested to his achievement.

I began truly to dislike this man, whom I henceforth dub "Secretary Mayo" to protect his anonymity. He did do me one favor. When we stopped at a tourist luncheonette, with buses crowded together like the Beijing motor pool, one of our handlers offered to fetch drinks for us. Encouraged by the assistant secretaries, almost everyone was up for a beer. But I had a raw, sore throat from the dust at the Wall and asked for hot tea. The handler responded, "You *would* have to be different."

His words somehow tweaked Mayo's nerve. For whatever reason—class status, ethnic assertiveness, or the remark's slam at American individualism—he said peremptorily, "I'll change my order to tea as well." Most of the others followed.

In our travels on this mission, we clung close to the coast, but we managed to accommodate George Hu's personal need to see his father's grave and then let him throw us all a party at his old Shanghai homestead. And we met the Chinese Communist Party's probable goal in bringing us to Shanghai—to show off its modernization and development. The plan was to return to Beijing in a few days after just a few days of sightseeing and meetings.

In Shanghai at a modest hotel, we were received by municipal leaders, including Dr. Zhang Zhong-li, who had been the head of the Shanghai Academy for Social Sciences and who had approved my invitation to do research there the previous year. "This is strange. What are you doing with this group?" he said to me on the side. I wondered.

George and his brother, who had made a bundle after returning to post-Maoist China, hosted a soiree to celebrate the interaction of the delegation with Chinese personalities of prominence. Not far from the place where a few men founded the Chinese Communist Party in 1921, and near the current U.S. Consulate, the house predated the revolution. Our first glance showed a small brick bungalow partly hidden in the dark shadows of foliage and tall, mechanized gates. Originally the servants' quarters, this was the place where George and his family had allegedly hidden below the rafters as the Cultural Revolution deepened, like Anne Frank in her Amsterdam abode.

Passing that little house, our bus rolled into a circular driveway covered with colored pebbles and bathed in pink lights that also shone on a three-story edifice—a fairytale house behind the dilapidated one, combining European and Chinese décor. The interior of this surreal stucco mansion included imitation Chinese antiques (dragons, Fu dogs, and the like), oak floors, an elevator, and a bandstand and dance floor.

The Hu brothers' guest list included well-known American businessmen, the president of Shanghai's famous Fudan University, the vice mayor of Shanghai, and a host of known dignitaries. Female students waited on all of us with drinks and hors d'oeuvres and otherwise engaged us visiting Americans, tête-à-tête, in banter and flirtation. Some of the young ladies at first seemed to be assigned to us individually, like hostesses at a Japanese bar.

A Chinese man who looked like he was in the movies started things moving in a room that had been set up for karaoke. I soon found myself singing along with a video of Elvis Presley as the vice mayor looked on. I felt strange in this Hollywood glitz, sheltered from the streets of Shanghai, where people straggled by out of work. State enterprises were closing and not paying their workers on time, and we were grabbing at appetizers catered by the Hilton. The Hu brothers had made no stylistic concessions to socialism.

At about half past nine, when I had begun to tire of these festivities, I decided to keep a tentatively scheduled appointment with my artist friend across town, the man who had accosted us when my wife and I were trying to find the Chinese artistic avant-garde. This time I was prepared to buy a good abstract painting. After informing the host of our delegation, Kirschner's counterpart on the Chinese side, I walked outside to hail a cab, a bit tipsy as I emerged from the pink lights.

What a delight to see my old acquaintance in his studio. He was working on a canvas and drew his brush across the painting with the smoothness of a figure skater. Nervous about violating protocol by leaving the party, I took odd comfort in his "undercover" role in public security, evident in the many coincidences surrounding our meeting, his earlier discussion of the tide of anti-foreign nationalism sweeping the country, and his deliberate effort to shepherd us here and there. But this time, when he took a break and pulled out some old photographs from his closet to show me, his smile seemed slightly malevolent. One framed photograph depicted his father, in 1950s military uniform, sitting with a group of People's Liberation Army senior officers surrounding Chairman Mao; the other was a dog-eared close-up of his dad, somewhat older, with his boot on the head of a dead American in North Vietnam. My friend had become both a Bohemian and a nationalist. Another dialectic contradiction!

After buying a large oil painting filled with Chinese mythical sea creatures and a bulbous penis drifting half-cocked in the waters, I went downstairs to find a cab. It was late, just before midnight. My friend Sun Liang saw several in the far distance riding slowly around a plaza circle. I gestured New York-style, and one taxi broke loose and headed our way. He pulled up in front of us, we maneuvered the painting into the back seat, and, waving goodbye to Sun Liang, I was whisked away.

"*Ni yao dao nali qiu?* (Where do you want to go)?" the driver asked, turning his head around.

I thought I'd better get back to the hotel at this hour, but I couldn't for the life of me remember the name of it. "Uh..."

After a dumb, attenuated pause from me, the driver blurted, "The Equatorial, isn't it?" With more than twenty million people in greater Shanghai, the cabbie somehow knew where to take me.

The next morning, we headed out to Pudong, the new foreign industrial zone still under development. Pudong had been the old section of Shanghai before the war, full of poverty and every sort of seamy sin. The Japanese troops had billeted there, and migrant Jews, doing business or trapped en route to Europe and the U.S., were interned there in the forties.

When we got out of our vehicles, the new terrain was full of factories and office buildings (most then with Japanese names like "Mitsubishi") and construction in various stages almost to the horizon. Amid all the din and testing of man against the environment was an ornamental tower (a symbol or monument like our Statue of Liberty). We climbed and took the elevator to one of the highest floors. At a certain level in the clouds, a beautiful panel showed us how this edifice compared—it was the tallest in the world—to the Sears Tower, World Trade Center, and other icons of tower power. I could see the psychological need for this display but wondered whether it justified the investment. Leaving the site, I overheard the agricultural assistant secretary ask, "What are they trying to prove?"

The defense assistant secretary responded, "One day, I know we'll be fighting them!"

As we prepared to leave Pudong, the mayor of Pudong and simultaneous vice mayor of Shanghai, an elderly man who had poked his head in on my singing the night before and with whom I had made some small bit of conversation, greeted us at the reception center and presented each of us with a commemorative gift. We had to see a movie—but a short one—about Pudong. I was surprised that the former assistant secretary of state for agriculture had nothing to say about the recruitment of farmers from the villages to serve as labor in this massive industrial undertaking, a policy that raised questions about both exposure to social dislocation and the imbalance of modernization. I enjoyed this session with the heads of Pudong and, in the silence that might have constituted Q. and A., I had a lively discussion with the mayor.

As we got up to leave, I asked him if my expressing some of my concerns about China's ability to absorb the speed of modernization disturbed him. "You know," he said, "I understood all your comments about what we are doing and about the risks, David. You should know that we already know that you are a friend of China." I was moved to tears by this redeeming gesture on the part of a Chinese leader.

As we pushed on to two or three economic, banking (CITIC), and political meetings, I was able to gain more of a psychological perspective on the Chinese style of dealing at this stage with hard-nosed foreigners and conservative Republicans. The central bankers and leading government economists informally answered, with clever jabs, at least two of the concerns of the assistant secretaries. "Restore the balance of payments?" asked one senior ministerial person rhetorically. "In view of your participation in the imperialist exploitation of China in the last century and your gunboat diplomacy, you owe us at least this much to catch up. Eventually the financial contradictions will resolve themselves to the benefit of us all. We need the United States to continue to invest in China's growth as it committed to us at the outset."

Stammering over this remark and similar ones, former Assistant Secretary Mayo demanded, "What about guaranteeing repatriation of our businessmen's capital and profits?"

"Ah," said another Chinese technocrat, who looked cosmopolitan and reminded me of one of the urbane Chinese intellectuals whom I admired in positions of authority in the U.S. "We want to be fair and encourage investment. What we say to your successful investors here is: 'Reinvest! Take your profits and diversify here. Build new buildings with money earned in China and reap a greater profit still.'"

The flustered leaders of our delegation toned down their remarks to a whimper. Now, they remained very tame about Taiwan's independence, and about Iran and North Korea.

The next day, when we got back to Beijing by train, the leaders of my delegation were moody. Kirschner informed me *in sotto voce* that the Chinese side had threatened to cancel our appointments unless he could talk me into assuming a passive role. The assistant secretary of state for agriculture led me to the rear corner of the hotel dining room, where he pointed to the lighting fixture above us. "Be careful what you say!" he whispered. I couldn't have cared less who heard us. He told me that the Chinese officials felt that I asked too many questions. I suggested that perhaps their security people, not the officials themselves, were being overprotective: I hadn't said anything very controversial, and my debating of issues was in the clear spirit of respect for Chinese Communists' thinking.

The assistant secretary, burning red in the face, screamed at me that in the remaining day or two, certain officials whom we were slated to see might withdraw from their interview commitments unless I promised to keep still. I actually agreed to assume a somewhat lower profile. Then Mayo gave me a start. After noting that I had written a lot and was known for my writing, he said he hoped I would write neither article nor book about this particular political mission upon my return. Startling even myself, I shouted, "I will publish what, where, and when I choose!"

"We will need to see everything first," he said.

"That wasn't my understanding," I said. "I'm not even under contract yet."

"Then you, my friend," he said, "will never work again!"

"Are you crazy? Who are you to keep me from ever finding work?"

"Well, at least you won't work for the Republicans."

"Well, there's a good chance of that," I sneered.

Again he pointed up at the light above the table. Standing up and walking about, I continued, "You're not too far from a society that plants mikes under every lamp, sir! You haven't listened to me even though I've spent years studying China. You haven't even taken my friendly advice in looking over old jade and porcelain pieces for yourself. You're the leader all right—of George Orwell's animal farm."

I had indeed fallen from grace, but I doubted that it had much to do with the Chinese opinion of my contribution. My fellow Americans were gagging me—on a mission that I had helped to arrange. Once or twice, I passed by the assistant secretary of state for defense talking with a Chinese general across a small table in the dining room. *He* was able to speak freely. I diverted myself from the pressure to keep silent at meetings, and from my own lingering fear that some of the Chinese might indeed have objected to me, by buying art from another contemporary painter. As it turned out, the smaller meetings at the end of our sojourn were cancelled anyway.

As our visit wound to a close, I became excited about the capstone meeting in the Great Hall of the People in Tiananmen Square with the vice chairman of the National People's Congress. The vice chairman sat in the deepest part of the large anteroom, and the rest of us formed a circle to his right. Kirschner sat next to the assistant secretary of state for agriculture, and I sat to the side of Kirschner. I believe the assistant secretary of state for defense was closest to the Chinese host but a little to the rear of him.

I sat quietly as the leaders on both sides schmoozed about collecting art and how the vice chairman had made a fortune for the government in Hong Kong before its integration into China. Then I sat back screwing my buttocks into the chair as I endured one inanity after another from former Assistant Secretary Mayo. I don't recall the defense person saying much at all. "This guy we selected is a jerk," I whispered in Kirschner's ear. "We could have done better."

"I agree that he can be," answered Kirschner with some indifference.

As Mayo's questions grew increasingly embarrassing, I repeated softly, but perhaps enunciating too clearly, "What a jerk!"

Mayo pushed aside his chair. "I can't take this," he shouted, and vaulted from the chamber. The Chinese vice chairman looked dumbfounded and then called angrily to his aides for a clarification. A couple of us shook the vice chairman's hand and followed the flow to the exit.

I wish I could remember more detail from the actual meeting. All that remains in my mind is the motorcade that followed, which split in parts and then reconstituted itself like the worms we played with as children. As we got back into our cars, we sped—all five cars, three times—around the grand circle at the entrance. On the fourth go-around, the rear cars parked on a far shoulder of the circle, while the first and second cars continued to spin around like an electric train. The former assistant secretary of state for agriculture—in the lead car—had ducked out of his car and entered the building. Instead of making a simple exit through the driveway, the remaining cars continued to gain speed around the circle—around and around. Four of the five original cars poured out the gated drive into Tiananmen Square and parked at the back side of the Great Hall of the People, each little black car, motor turned off, several yards from the next.

Silence. I was cold and hungry.

I sat shivering in part from the cold wind, in part from anxiety. Alone in the rear seat of my Red Flag limousine, I reflected that at some point I must have resolved to discredit both the delegation and the not-for-profit that we claimed to represent. I didn't want the Chinese government to take this sham outfit seriously. And yet I also wondered whether the Chinese weren't simply using it to generate reciprocal visits, particularly to Washington, that might bring them into closer personal touch with the real opinion-makers on the political right in the U.S.

If only I had better self-esteem, I thought, I wouldn't be so provocative. "I'm glad the Chinese know I mean well," I muttered to myself. Brimming with angst and needing to unburden myself, I turned to the driver, who I guessed had a double role, and asked him in Chinese if I could tell him what had happened. For the moment, he would also play psychotherapist. Recapitulating the interplay at the meeting, I suggested that the delegation leaders were not powerful players, and that they had made no apparent effort to educate themselves about post-revolutionary China.

The driver smiled and said, "I see that you are upset."

We waited. I got out of the car without an overcoat and felt empowered by wintry gusts in my face. Ahead, pacing back and forth, I saw Kirschner. He knew nothing except that the assistant secretary seemed to have been called in to make an apology. "I don't know if we're going to have that parting banquet here after all," he added.

"Well, it's late," I said.

As I walked back toward my car, I mumbled, "I don't think I want to be anyone's stooge any longer." I told the driver that I could no longer stay under these circumstances. "Nice talking with you."

With a sad, quizzical look, he protested, "Oh, only little while." Nevertheless, I got out of the car again, walked toward the surrounding roadway and hailed a taxi for the hotel, where I postponed eating and took a soft chair in the front of the lobby facing the doors.

They didn't arrive together, as I recall. The first in was the defense specialist. He grinned at me. "They cancelled the dinner," he said.

"There's food upstairs," I said. "If you'll take my suggestion, I recommend the noodles."

The delegation heads were supposed to stay on in China a few days more to do some personal business on their own. I didn't really see Assistant Secretary Mayo at all until I noticed that he was actually aboard the same flight as the group. I imagined that he had rendered some sort of apology to the vice chairman of the National People's Congress and had been asked to leave.

Once we were airborne, he signaled that he wanted to speak to me, and I followed him to the kitchen nook in business class. He mumbled, almost inaudibly, "Wait," and pulled a scrap of paper out of his pocket. He startled me with his jerky movements. He proceeded to scribble on it with an urgency that was confusing. "I'm sorry for the way I acted. But we *needed* the Chinese to stick with us."

I stared quizzically at him, not knowing what to say.

CHAPTER EIGHT

2011

REFLECTIONS

I never really intended to wreck havoc in China. It possibly was more a question of my self-centeredness. I felt that because I had devoted so much time to the study of China's language (classical and modern), culture, history, politics and extraneous embroidery (all in the way I imagined it), I would never be disappointed with this country. After all, this culture had a sophisticated, enduring presence more than 3,000 years earlier.

But when I finally got to China after watching its orchestrated social convulsions from another continent for years after the revolution, I was disappointed. I expected that the rigid hierarchy would have been battered and shaken loose a little. I imagined that these larger-than-life Chinese also should have been more aware of *me*. A relatively small number of us were monitoring the new China. Wasn't I entitled to some special acknowledgment when I actually set foot on Communist Chinese soil?

I admit to being a little narcissistic. As years passed and I gained real exposure to different parts and sectors of China, I developed a sort of love–hate relationship with the Chinese. If someone or some organization let me down or sideswiped my idealized expectations of them, I felt that I had the right to take action. Even if the Chinese conformed to what I had thought about their predilections and social structure, I eventually came to make value judgments according to what I felt should be universal standards. In this respect, I trailed only a little behind the human rights advocates in this country whose constituency here had widened to include both of our political parties and a good share of China specialists as well. I used to defend China's sovereignty over most of what we considered abuses of human rights: its choice of whom to arrest, their incarceration of citizens without pretense of what we consider "due process;" ethnic cleansing of the Uighurs in the northwestern province of Xinjiang and abuses in the interrogation process. I gradually became critical of their infringements on the U.N. Declaration of Human Rights and developed countries' interpretation of individual freedom. This may well have been related to their criticism of my bad experiences taking liberties over there. Was decorum more important to the Chinese than business? And was I more sensitive to constraints on individual freedoms than the Chinese were themselves?

My life and China's seemed interwoven. I showed my displeasure and reacted in a personal way, and I held those oppressive Chinese authorities at different levels accountable for their interference. I chafed at their "rudeness" and doubled-up on my own propensity to confront and be gruffly resistant. So many things got under my skin: the social hierarchy, authoritarian and unyielding attitudes toward those of lower status in the work unit, lack of self-initiative, rigid conformity to rules and norms, unwillingness to confront an adversary or contrary argument, hypocritical politeness followed by a stab in the back, intolerance of straying from the group or from arrangements planned for the agenda, and my trepidations over every independent move that I considered undertaking in China. In their negative effects, these impediments were like winter snow chains on wheels. They ground on me and seemed like personal harassments. I reacted negatively and even tried to resist and defy.

The absence of an ideology that could provide a sense of direction, socially conscious habits and legitimacy for the Communist regime left a vacuum that even the Communist Party wanted to fix. Given the muddied waters of the post-Mao ideology by1996, the Party Central Committee finally set down a list of hollow behavioral standards for Chinese to exercise in public. Such Communist homilies as, "From each according to his ability, to each according to his means," were put in the archives. Many of the values in a central committee draft predictably were about what not to do, but others addressed a positive concern for others. The Communist Party Ideology Department gave me a copy of the document. Spitting was not permitted in the street—a restriction that particularly one who has experienced a wind blowing in an unpredictable direction might appreciate.

One example in practice of the authorities' meddling from above concerned a sudden declaration from Unit Head Chen at the Shanghai Academy of Social Sciences. Midway through my formal interview work using a tape recorder, he announced that he should either have my recordings transcribed for me or preferably copy my cassettes. Early the next morning, I was really anxious about confiscation or censorship and whipped myself into frenzy. I hailed a cab to the U.S. Consulate in a loud voice and with a sense of crisis gripping my body. I noticed the hotel doorman react to me, running in the opposite direction. With an apology that she didn't have the "fast, express" machine, the CIA chief of station at the Consulate agreed to have copies made of all my tapes before the day was done. Of course, the U.S. Central Intelligence Agency would be able now to stash away a set of its own. The CIA official spoke to me in a combination of whisper and mumble to mask her words from eavesdroppers—everywhere. And I followed her cues.

I felt like I was behind enemy lines. A lot of the personal orders handed down from Chinese in authority inside and outside the Academy were harsher because of the tone in which they were administered.

I withstood most reprimands and reversals of decision. In contrast, some of my friends among the Chinese told me that *they* never noticed any particular demands or reproaches from above in their work or daily lives. They even resisted the notion of being in the shadow of public security surveillance. Were they being candid with me, or was it a sort of unconscious *denial* resulting from their socialization?

I surely did feel the oppressiveness, as did the Americans and other Westerners at the airport departure lounge on each trip. Western tourists generally showed their relief, sometimes cheering, as they boarded their planes for overseas.

As an American, self-centered and adventurous, I was sensitive to the authoritarian nature of Chinese mainland society both in the family and in the work unit—extending to what I considered public and private areas of behavior. Americans in particular tend to take for granted a certain amount of independence in their lives, usually from adolescence onward. As an adult, I was even more allergic to the personalized use of authority. I had experienced a tough and rage-filled upbringing from my father and parental manipulation. I felt that I had to fight for my autonomy. And I looked for the syndrome in others and other societies. Politics was usually only an overlay.

Years later when I met Chinese in the U.S. who had distanced themselves in time and space from the China that they had experienced as youth, I heard how abrasive and punitive the hierarchy really had become for them in China. They all declared that they had made it out "chu lai" of the mainland China system. They recalled the precise date. They confided that whether at work or play, in the Party or larger social environment, expressing opinions—especially political or anti-collective innuendo—had been dangerous. Similarly, an individualistic flourish in their work had always been subject to question. And failure to obey an authority or supervisor had been virtually unconscionable. The Communist dictatorship in reality was simply a different superstructure resting on a *traditional* social matrix. Ordinary people got so accustomed to it that they internalized it—*more or less*—and could make comparisons or seem to change a bit only away from the source and interacting with cultural strangers.

The China that I describe—in a transition from Maoist communism to modernity—accepts as reality the viability in practice of a combination of socialist dictatorship and capitalist characteristics. "Socialist dictatorship" and economic capitalism are often taken to constitute a dialectical contradiction, like *Yin* and *Yang*. People can live with contradictions. We are not accustomed to seeing the two systems complement one another, but they can work together with adaptation to the special dynamics of a society like China's. These conjoined economic, political and social systems are effective now for China not primarily because they are a logical fit but because they operate reasonably well together, managing to maintain *order and avoid much-feared chaos.*

CONFUSION, DEMOCRATIZATION OR THE CHINESE WAY

Historically in China, when authority has been in disarray and an overarching ideology seems to fail, social order crumbles and "brings down the house." Increased modernization since the 1970s (physical and financial rather than political) hangs in the balance. Should there be few major social disruptions in the future, China stands to do more than catch up with the industrial West.

With the explosion of burgeoning "democratic" yearnings on the part of a segment of the young elite who demonstrated at Tiananmen and in Chinese cities other than Beijing in spring-summer 1989, the government became circumspect and tightened its grip. A major Communist policy reversal was to stamp out the seedlings of democracy during the more relaxed 1980s. Deng Xiaoping became more of a recidivist and strived to maintain and fortify the vertical social pyramid. A non-party election in a university was invalidated, sending the successful candidate sometime later to Queens, New York.

Uneven economic development, a crisis in the state ideology and *chaos* or freedom run amuck seem to have been regarded as key threats to China's reassertion of its steadfast culture in the postmodern world. More people in the world take notice now of China's embedded corruption, privilege of the upper class (Party, corporate and overseas Chinese), traditionally ingrained class abuses, colonial-like spread of Chinese influence in the third world and adeptness at their own public relations in different countries. This new generation also exhibits haughtiness with foreign visitors—the result of pride over a newfound economic grip on the world. In this reassertion of status as a nation and culture, one sees the arrogance that accompanies a major comeback. When democracy again begins to emerge at the grassroots level in an electoral contest with a self-selected, non-party candidate, the Party leadership runs interference. And the government's use of coercion and internment to cope with dissidents expands as it meets resistance. Its response to resistance from the world: to maintain a face of imperviousness.

It puzzles me that so many of us "China experts" have been hopeful that the People's Republic of China would become more participatory and democratic following the decline of Maoism. My professors from Columbia as well as I tried to trace patterns of institutional reform at the lowest levels. Through observation, survey and impressionistic interviewing, we have explored family openness in childhood and leaks in the "great wall" of silence during those times.

I wrote an early book—basically my doctoral dissertation, and using psychological interviewing as its core research—during the first years of the Cultural Revolution. I argued that families (particularly the more educated) were becoming increasingly permissive and egalitarian. Inclined to assert their autonomy, a conspicuous number of youths in adolescence were more apt to confront authorities immediately above them. Young people seemed to push harder to attain a place and voice in the adult society. Given the turbulence of one political movement following another in the wake of the Communist revolutionary victory in 1949, I don't think I was mistaken about this post-revolutionary trend. For twenty years, society remained shaken by a concatenation of cataclysms, culminating in the Great Proletarian Cultural Revolution at its most violent stage in the late 1960s. These shake-ups, often at all levels, tugged at filial piety at its roots and made many families more open. Maturing young people in the cities could fantasize, even plan, the way to assume more meaningful roles in adult society.

These tremors served to undo vertical ties in society and rattled the social system. The post-revolutionary generations were buffeted by the influence of peers, political study groups, and the technique of criticism and self-criticism to change behavior through group therapy-like sessions. Even the surface-like qualities of economic modernization and styles imported from the West (when I was there in the late 1990s, Michael Jackson was the music hero and now it appears that rap is the rage) have probably gnawed at the legitimacy of authorities in the family and beyond.

I think what we have observed in Chinese mainland society is the nascent growth of an openness in the family system that was reinforced later by more enlightened authorities — teachers, other adults and official authorities — outside the intimacy of the home. Even during the factional Red Guard fighting of the Cultural Revolution, one observed certain segments of the youth and workers breaking through the long-enduring pattern of an authority-submissive society. When the Cultural Revolution created disorder in the schools and streets at the end of the 1960s, teenagers didn't necessarily explode in all directions. Often, they targeted in an individually subjective way those authorities who were kind but also stood in their way toward greater roles in adult society. Their criticism was directed against teachers who resembled their own liberal fathers but remained their teachers and adult overseers. These father figures encouraged open discussion and emphasized hope for the students' success in the society at large. Like the fathers of these youth, the authority-surrogates were pointing the way to position and success. In their *transference,* these same young educated Chinese would often perceive their favorite teachers as objects of struggle, identifying them with their fathers. This phenomenon represented a building block for the sort of directed political participation that could have characterized a more responsibly democratic system later. And indeed in the 1980s, at least in the more exposed modern sector, we could detect a discernible openness and democracy. But outside cheerleaders for democratic modernization went a bit too far in their optimism concerning both adult positive reinforcement in the wider society and the timing of the anticipated bottom-up ferment and openness at the family and grassroots societal levels. The *evolution* away from the millennia-old, traditional structure and dynamics of Chinese society did not appear to be linear. Hence, twenty-five years into the future, reflecting on a different past during the politically turbulent period, a taxi driver with whom I talked in Beijing remembered the violent first years of the Cultural Revolution as "the *freest* period — the best period — in my life." In the denouement of the Cultural Revolution, young people had their first experience in the action of subjective and self-motivated participation.

To explain what happened, authorities came under attack during the Cultural Revolution, and for a long while there were no authorities around. Adolescents formed factions — all of them trying to prove themselves the staunchest protagonists for Mao Zedong in different ways. They fought with one another in the streets through street bulletins, and in factional fights with blades inserted in the toes of their shoes. They even removed handguns from People's Liberation Army officers (another form of authority) to use against rival groups. When the more active part of the Cultural Revolution ebbed and became routinized after 1969, students who had harbored glorious dreams for themselves and China were not elevated but sent to rustic areas for corrective steeling. And the rest of the segments of the population seemed to go back to sleep.

By 1976, the "Great Proletarian Cultural Revolution"

period was declared at an end. The militant "Gang of Four" was discredited and soon buried. Urban youth who had been torn from their school routine and sent into the "wilderness" for a lifetime of toil began to make their way back to home cities or urban areas where they had relatives. Henceforth, we would all be looking over our shoulders at the age of mass movement. "A revolution in a test tube," Mao had proclaimed. Its icons: the little red book, the Red Guards, Mao statues and pins, the spilled blood of groups of teens fighting one another, political activism and backstabbing, suicides, and bodies floating in the rivers. Stillness ensued and people took their proper place at work and in society.

Many of the young educated found jobs or proceeded with their schooling in the cities. Parents often stayed indoors and warned their children to show reserve and be careful. Those who returned to university were said to have shunned politics as much as possible. They had apparently learned the hard way and further advised others, like their younger brothers and sisters. A certain demureness in classrooms now seemed deliberate.

The ultimate deterrent to group political action befell the next generation of youth who camped out in Tiananmen Square in May-June 1989, knowing they might be at risk of bodily harm. The supreme leader, Deng Xiaoping, had tolerated considerable political openness in Chinese universities for a decade. The young university students who began marching on May Fourth (which historically had been a day to celebrate youth) attracted workers, younger people and general sympathizers in their occupation of the square. They succeeded in putting their demands before the highest officials of the land, and they were rebuffed. The inevitable doom lay in the simple fact that their *demands* were just so, *demands from below*.

Now, in the first part of the third millennium, cataclysms are more likely to be geological and environmental than political. The regime of Deng Xiaoping tolerated democratic reforms for a while as long as they remained mere sprouts at the grassroots. But when the participatory frustrations of youth erupted in Tiananmen Square in summer 1989, the government made a decisive choice not to put their power at risk. They couldn't afford to listen to the young student leaders. At stake for China's top political elite was "loss of face" and legitimacy in the appearance of capitulation to children and inferiors. And the end result, after all, indeed might be the much-dreaded chaos and disorder. The Tiananmen Massacre of 1989 appears to have set back the advance of any real democratization. The rehabilitated urban youth of an earlier generation and those later crushed at Tiananmen seemed to come to accept their places in the old-style, vertical society. And when it appeared that a non-Party candidate was elected yet again in 2011 at the grassroots, the Party cancelled the results.

As long as present and future generations of Chinese become accustomed to material progress, they will seek more intangibles. It is only human that they will want more in their lives. Perhaps, freedoms and democracy, bubble by bubble, will percolate to the surface over time and ultimately encounter a more confident leadership. I would wager that any real democratization would take the form of a so-called *subject* civic culture, a system with a popular vote and participation but characterized by a strong leadership or symbolically strong leader at the top and a comparatively deferential people below.

What about free-spirited Americans and other Western visitors like me? Until a rigid hierarchy with one party at the top loosens its demands on the individual, Westerners who expect to be their own people working in China will feel constrained. For the foreigner who immerses himself a bit in the society, China is likely to seem less like a giant than a small, airtight box.

It might follow that we should anticipate the possibility of a clash of cultures between our nations. Many structural and behavioral issues are at stake that are potential sources of friction and open conflict. The West, particularly the U.S., places emphasis on the individual and on human rights more these days as ends in themselves rather than for political leverage. The Chinese government is at odds with our concept of human rights or equal rights as long as it seems to threaten the state. Chinese in authority generally discourage and are repelled by what they deem to be individualism and individualism in others. Rebels against the state are pariahs, or still treated like "non-people." Since the revolution, the Party has had various pejorative terms for what we praise as "individualism."

As I prepare for one more trip to the People's Republic of China, I already understand myself better and am ready for a more realistic interaction with the Chinese.

ABOUT THE AUTHOR

David M. Raddock received his doctorate from Columbia University in Chinese politics and political culture and is author of *Political Behavior of Adolescents in China* and several books on international political risk. He was formerly international political director in the Washington office of ENSERCH Corporation and a senior research associate at Columbia University. He founded and coordinated the Country Affairs Group among corporate offices in Washington in the 1980s. Later, he was a consultant to presidential candidates Carlos Andres Perez of Venezuela and Daniel Ortega Saavedra of Nicaragua. He has a working knowledge of the Chinese, Russian, and French languages.

Raddock now enjoys writing articles on contemporary Chinese art and has garnered a wide collection of modern and contemporary Chinese and Western art. He makes his home these days in Boulder, Colorado.

www.ingramcontent.com/pod-product-compliance
Lightning Source LLC
Chambersburg PA
CBHW030949090426
42737CB00007B/552